Once Upon a Country Road

Once Upon a Country Road

Ruth Busbee Smith

XULON PRESS

Xulon Press
2301 Lucien Way #415
Maitland, FL 32751
407.339.4217
www.xulonpress.com

© 2022 by Ruth B. Smith

All rights reserved solely by the author. The author guarantees all contents are original and do not infringe upon the legal rights of any other person or work. No part of this book may be reproduced in any form without the permission of the author.

Due to the changing nature of the Internet, if there are any web addresses, links, or URLs included in this manuscript, these may have been altered and may no longer be accessible. The views and opinions shared in this book belong solely to the author and do not necessarily reflect those of the publisher. The publisher therefore disclaims responsibility for the views or opinions expressed within the work.

Unless otherwise indicated, Scripture quotations taken from the King James Version (KJV)–*public domain*.

Paperback ISBN-13: 978-1-66284-305-1
Ebook ISBN-13: 978-1-66284-306-8

Dedicated to my dear husband, friend, and encourager
Owen J. Smith

Table of Contents

Introduction ix

PART 1: PERSONALITIES 1

1. My Parents – Andrew Jackson Busbee
   and Crosia Sharpe Busbee 3

2. Hillary Pet (H. P.) Busbee
   and Floyd Marion Busbee 9

3. Horace Elisha Busbee, Dorcas "Dot" Rachael Hayden,
   and Ezra "Buzzie" Nathaniel Busbee 15

4. David Jeremiah Busbee, Esther Mae Raines Williams,
   and Nellie Ruth Smith 23

5. Lois Crosia Moore
   and Hosea Andrew "Tracy" Busbee 33

PART 2: EDUCATION AND FUN 41

6. Educational Opportunities 43
7. Fun and Play 55

PART 3: MY HOME AND HOMETOWN 61

8. House and Surroundings 63
9. Downtown Swansea 73

Part 4: Activities of Daily Living LARGE 83
10. Clothing a BIG family 85
11. Seating a Houseful 91

Part 5: The Things We Take for Granted 95
12. Utilities or Lack Thereof 97
13. Keeping Warm or Cool 105
14. The Prized Appliances 115

Part 6: Farm Life 123
15. Farming for Cash and Cuisine 125
16. Tools of the Trade 149
17. Food from the Barnyard 157
18. Growing and Preserving 171

Part 7: Blessing in Disguise 191
19. Rewards of Growing Up without Much Stuff 193

Afterthoughts 197
Acknowledgments 205

Introduction

THIS BOOK IS my vantage point of country living in the 1940s and 1950s. Growing up in the country during the 1940s and the 1950s was a continual adventure. On a crisp October morning, a bouncing baby girl was born to Andrew and Crosia Sharpe Busbee. I was the eighth child among five older brothers and two sisters. Another sister and a brother were born later.

All of us were born at home in Lexington County, South Carolina. We children were close knit in those early years. Because we had little extra money, most of our food was raised on the farm. There were few bought toys. We learned to create our playthings and used our imaginations to come up with new games. We built a playhouse in the woods and used a diversity of objects for furniture and dishes. The innovative approach to creating childhood recreation has been carried forward into my adult life.

When I was a child, a typical day began around six o'clock in the morning with everyone seated around a long table with benches on each side. Each of us sat at an assigned place for each meal. Everyone ate breakfast. Our breakfast consisted of grits, eggs, some homegrown meat, biscuits, and milk or water. I was sixteen before I realized that everyone did not eat grits. After breakfast we all pitched in to do the chores before school. Each of us had something to do. Someone cleared the table. Others fed the livestock, chickens, and pigs, while someone milked the cow. Then off to school we went in the fall, winter, and spring. In the summer, off to the fields and garden we went. My work habits today are reflective of my childhood training.

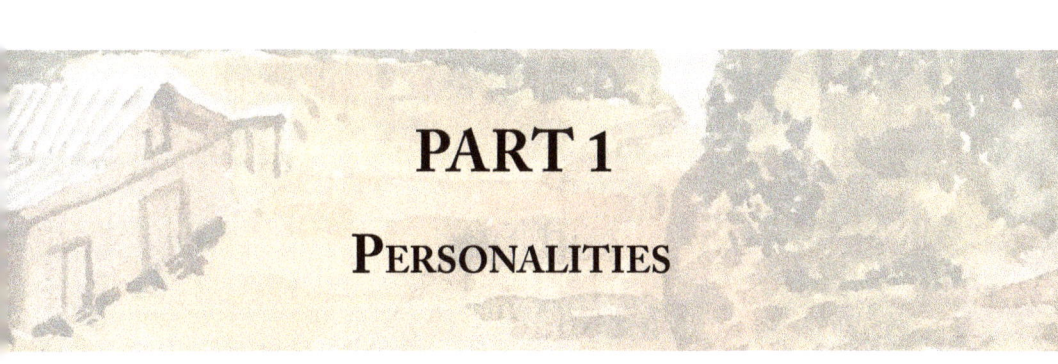

PART 1

PERSONALITIES

Chapter 1

My Parents Andrew Jackson Busbee and Crosia Sharpe Busbee

Dad

Andrew Jackson Busbee was the product of a blended family, born September 9, 1892, to Aaron and Nancy Harsey Busbee. His father's first wife died, and they had three children—Mary, Lucy, and John Thomas. Dad's mother also had a son named Haskell Harsey. The two parents gave birth to Andrew Jackson and Robert Franklin.

Although my records indicate there were two other children, Dorley and Hattie Pearl Busbee, who may have died young, because I don't remember hearing anything about them. Dad was close to his sister Mary, and her husband, Arthur Sharpe, and their children.

His face was square, with blue-gray eyes and an olive complexion. His hair was brown. It is interesting to compare reality to what I thought back then. For example, I thought Dad was tall. In reality he was only five feet, nine inches. To me, he was strong, although he weighed no more than 140 pounds. Perhaps it was his strong will and loud voice that created those perceptions.

Although Dad was strong willed and stern, I believe he had a tender heart, because I saw him cry a number of times. As the head of his house, Dad's decision was always the final one in our home, and he handled almost all of the discipline in our family. All children deserve parents who love and are willing to train them, and all of us respected him from day one. My daddy was probably the most influential person in my life, although my attributes and characteristics are a combination of both parents.

Dad's authority was never questioned. Whatever he asked the children to do, we did. He believed the old adage, "Those who don't work, don't eat." Each of us was assigned chores to complete from a young age. hose work habits instilled in me as a child still prevail today. It is difficult to sit idly by and do nothing. I am constantly doing something.

Another fond memory is my dad reading to us around the open fireplace. This was a regular routine and planted a thirst for knowledge. It was a challenge to open new arenas.

One day, when I was fairly young, Mom sent me to the field to carry water to Dad. His actions are so vivid in my mind. Sitting on his plow while drinking his water, he related to me the Bible story of Noah and the Ark. A rainbow came alive in my young mind. This event only touches the tip of the story-telling iceberg. Whatever he read, he shared with enthusiasm.

Dad loved to play his old upright organ with foot pedals and sing, whether alone or with the family as a group. As noted throughout this book, most of the Busbee family had musical talent. Eight of his ten children played one or more musical instrument, and many of the grandchildren are very talented musically.

My dad had an abundance of faith and believed in the power of prayer. As a little girl, I wanted to be near him if I was sick or upset. Although

I knew he could not fix or solve my problems, his strength helped me. Children need parents who teach life's values by example as my dad did. Throughout my life, I respected my parents and tried to never bring shame or disgrace to their reputation.

Mom

Born Crosia Sharpe, my mother was the fourth child of Daniel "Ad" Adam Sharpe and Isabelle Sarah Sharpe Sharpe. You read that correctly—*two* "Sharpes"—since both of Grandmother Sharpe's parents had that last name before marriage. She was born August 7, 1898. Mom had three older siblings, Daniel, John, and Catherine Sharpe (Hoover). Following Mom were sisters Gertrude (Sightler, Backman), Mervelle (Sturkie), and Viney (Sightler), and brother Otis Sharpe.

Mom was reared outside the small town of Gaston, South Carolina, and enjoyed relating stories about riding a buggy to Harmony Baptist Church where many of her relatives are buried.

Mom and Dad were married May 14, 1916, when she was seventeen years old. She and Dad had six sons and four daughters, raising us on a farm three miles outside of Swansea, South Carolina, on Jones Wire Road in Lexington County. My dad inherited this property from his mother's family. Samuel Harsey owned many acres.

A common characteristic of the Sharpe family was very blue eyes and fair complexion. Mom was no exception, about five feet, three inches tall. I am told she was thin when younger. However, I always remember her as plump, probably caused by a thyroid problem, which was diagnosed in her early seventies.

Quiet and extremely gentle, Mom lived without guile. Disciplining her children was very difficult, and she never spanked me, although, corporal punishment was quite acceptable in that day. When it came to punishment, I can almost hear her saying now "Wait until your daddy gets home." I recall that she loved to sing, including to her babies. Even into her autumn years, she would sing old hymns with my dad.

Her workload must have been difficult. She cooked on a wood-burning stove making biscuits and corn bread every day. There was no automatic washing machine, just a washpot and scrub board for doing laundry. The very first thing I bought, on credit, when I went to work, was a washing machine for her. Clothing the children must have been a real chore.

Mom loved all of her children. Often, she would tell her friends or relatives that all of us were pretty. Whenever someone would question her about an older sibling's selfishness or manipulative traits, she would respond that it was because that child had to go through the Great Depression, even though Mom was not at all inclined to be that way.

Mom was as honorable as the most prestigious woman. I tried to never do anything to bring shame or hurt to her great worth. She told me, "Children walk on your feet when they are little but on your heart when they are bigger."

Dad with A-Model Ford

Dad with me
Before my wedding

Dad in 1949
Hudson car

Mom & Dad in mid-50s

Mom In her twenties

Mom in the
mid-50s

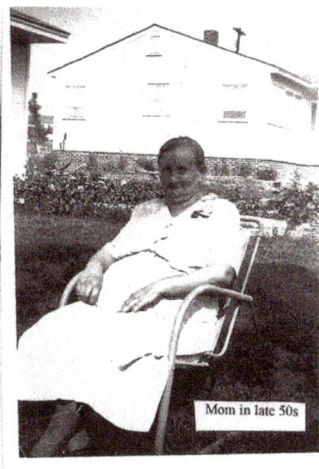
Mom in late 50s

Chapter 2

HILLARY PET (H. P.) BUSBEE AND FLOYD MARION BUSBEE

The Oldest Sibling

HILLARY PET (H.P.) Busbee was born in Lexington County, South Carolina, on October 11, 1921, the oldest of ten children. I cannot remember his living at home with us.

In January 1940, H. P. was married to Annie Lee Wise, and their first child, Annie Pearl, was born and died before Hosea, our youngest brother, was born. The second daughter, Sarah, was born in October 1942. Since she was ten months younger than our youngest brother, it became quite confusing when they went to the same school and attended some of the same classes. Three other children, Helen, Robert, and Paul, were born to H. P. and Annie Lee in the 1940s. James Talmadge was born in 1950.

Blue-eyed, H. P. carried himself well, around six feet tall and a slender 165–170 pounds. With light brown hair, not as dark as mine, I think that H. P. looked more like Dad's side of the family.

He and his family lived in Columbia when I first remember him. However, they soon moved near our home on Martin-Neese Road, when our dad gave him some acreage at the intersection of Jones Wire Road. He built his home and remained there all his life. We saw him frequently, since H. P.'s family lived within a half-mile, during my growing-up years. My sisters and I seemed to be built-in babysitters for his children.

Mom told me that H. P. worked for the WPA (Works Progress Administration), the government program started by President Franklin D. Roosevelt during the Great Depression. He was really tight with his money and never seemed to splurge on anything, even on himself. This must have been a difficult period for everyone. The WPA workers made community improvements, including drainage ditches, roads, and community center construction, such as the Swansea Community House on U.S. Hwy #321 (log building).

Some people thought that H. P. would have made an excellent lawyer, because he always knew the facts and could argue his cases. For example, he always seemed to know how to get whatever he wanted from our parents! He traded Dad an old car for some prime land to build a pond.

During my junior and senior high school years, I worked in Columbia on the weekends. H. P. was kind to pick me up from school and take me to meet Floyd at the Olympia Pacific Mill. They worked different shifts in the same factory.

On Saturday nights, I rode to Swansea with him. It seemed like he enjoyed selling almost anything. Many times he helped me sell candy, gadgets, and magazines to raise money for school projects. I probably got to know him better during this time frame than any other period.

While playing the guitar, H. P. liked to sing Southern Gospel music. He would be sure to attend if there was a "singing" nearby. Other hobbies included hunting, fishing, gardening, and coin collecting. In his later years, he was a big flea market fan and probably made a bit of money with his dickering or horse trading, as some "rednecks" would say.

The Second Brother

Floyd Marion Busbee was born August 7, 1923, on Mom's birthday. He grew to six feet, always standing tall and trim and weighing 170 pounds at most. With very blue eyes, blond hair, and Mom's fair complexion, many people called him "Blondie." Yet, he never seemed to mind since the young ladies liked his looks and most people thought he was quite handsome!

My earliest recollection is that he worked as an electric welder at Columbia's Pacific Cotton Mill. He lived at our home and left for work around 6 a.m. Mom woke him daily, cooked breakfast, and packed a lunch for him. It was around 4 p.m. when he got home.

Floyd paid a lot of attention to the younger siblings. For example, we did not go to the dentist for regular check-ups, only when there was a big problem like the abscessed tooth I experienced at about five years old. Floyd volunteered to take me, since he had already bought his first car at about nineteen or twenty years of age. What a vivid memory! I was scared when my tooth had to be extracted, yet he was so strong and kind, offering to buy me anything I wanted. This was my first and last time that I received a man's offer to give me whatever I wished. The result was a bunch of bananas, which was shared with the others.

Ineligible for the World War II draft due to asthma, he was required by the U.S. government to build ships in Pensacola, Florida. He served several years there before returning to South Carolina.

On March 15, 1944, Floyd and Edna Frances Fallaw from Monetta, South Carolina, were married. We not only gained a sister-in-law, but a trusted friend and encourager. Although only seventeen at the time, she spent a lot of time with Lois, Hosea, and me. Both of them did special things for us, taking us places that we would not have gone otherwise.

Their only son, Francis Marion, was born December 15, 1946, and more or less grew up with us. I have precious memories shared with him. Floyd liked fishing and was an avid hunter, spending his spare time hunting rabbits, squirrels, and birds. Later, he hunted deer as a hunt club member. He was passionate about sports, including boxing, football, baseball, and racing. Gifted in music, he and Edna often sang together. Floyd played the guitar, mandolin, and banjo. Both were excellent teachers at Northside Baptist Church in West Columbia, South Carolina.

While I am sure that Floyd had faults, he was the most generous and helpful person I have ever known. No matter the circumstance, I knew I could depend on him when the going got tough. Throughout his life, he referred to me as his "kid sister." He was my hero, and I loved him dearly. Dr. J. O. Reed, Jr. wrote a poem in honor of Floyd at his death.

A Tribute to Floyd

"Let the children come to me," words of Jesus plain to see
In the lives of Floyd and Edna demonstrated eternally.
Tears of sadness, tears of joy, were so plentiful in this country boy.

He loved his pastor, loved his church, in the boat he found his perch
To enjoy the lake and the blue sky, and bring home fish to fry.

From ancestors busy as a bee, came the name Busbee, it's plain to see.
Floyd was one to bear it well, of the family he loved to tell.

Never too busy to lend a hand, to help a poor widow move her stuff, and give hope to those who had it tough.

A good team player day by day, even if it wasn't quite the way
He might want to do the task, he had no beg favor for which to ask.

His yard was a veritable paradise, with shrubs and flowers
and luscious grass. His house by the road was good to pass.

Though some may wonder what to say, or where to stand on this or that.
Floyd left no doubt about his love on God's side he would stand pat.

Object of God's amazing grace, he made proud the human race.
Friend of all who came his way, he shared Jesus day by day.

Thank you, Edna, for all you've done, to care for Floyd from sun to sun.
At his side you found your place, with the Lord you both kept pace.
Now his work on earth is done, in spite of tears he had fun.

Though so serious he loved to tease, went out of his way to always please.
"To God be the glory" is epitaph, for one who traveled along the path.
Of seeking and finding and doing God's will,
In God's presence his hope fulfill.

Used by permission
Rev. John O. Reed, Jr.

Chapter 3

Horace Elisha Busbee, Dorcas "Dot" Rachael Hayden (née Busbee), and Ezra "Buzzie" Nathaniel Busbee

My Third Brother

Horace Elisha Busbee was born on November 12, 1925, the third child of Andrew and Crosia Busbee. Growing to about six feet tall and stocky, Horace had blue eyes, a fair complexion, and light brown hair. At about two hundred pounds, he was the family rebel, and I don't have many memories of his living at home. As our only sibling drafted into the military, the U.S. Army assigned him to Fort Bragg, NC, at age eighteen.

During the latter part of World War II, he served a tour of duty in Germany. I recall that my mother cried a lot while he was gone. At such a young age, I could not understand why. Stationed in Fort Sill, Oklahoma, after returning stateside, Horace later worked for Swansea Milling Company upon military discharge. Located on S.C. Highway 6 west of the business district, this plant made grits and cornmeal from corn grown in the area.

Horace and Valarie Hayden were married soon after he finished military service. The first of their four children, Horace Jr. (Ricky), was born in Swansea on August 17, 1949. After moving to Columbia/West Columbia, Horace and Valarie had three more children during the 1950s, while he worked at various jobs. The marriage fell apart, leaving his children to be raised by different family members. For a number of years our family had no contact with him before he eventually returned to South Carolina.

His hobbies included hunting and fishing. He had a nice singing voice and played the guitar, actually singing hymns on the radio in his sunset years. He liked to tape his music. I never felt that I really knew him.

My Oldest Sister

Dorcas "Dot" Rachael Hayden was the oldest daughter of Andrew and Crosia Sharpe Busbee, born on November 29, 1927. It is interesting to note that the oldest daughter was born on November 29 while years later the youngest daughter was born October 29. It seemed ironic that six of the ten siblings were born in October and November!

I was told that she was born a blonde, which seems reasonable since she looked a lot like our mother. My memory pictures her with blue eyes, brown hair, and a height of about five feet, three or four inches tall. She was never skinny, but not overly stout at about 140 pounds. Most everyone remembers her as a lovely girl.

My most prominent recollection, from the 1940s, is that she always smiled. Very pleasant and kind to the younger children, Dot's side of the story is that she helped raise us. It's probably true, although I did not know she felt that way until recently.

Dot could fix most anything and was handy with tools. From my earliest memory, she helped Mom cook breakfast. She surely could bake biscuits! One of her daily chores was to milk the cow, but we'll come back to that responsibility later. It seemed that Dorcas could do almost anything the guys could do; most likely, she learned from the older brothers. Horace could make her miserable as the target of many pranks, yet her patience was admirable, ever smiling.

Dorcas and Eroy Hayden were married on May 14, 1948, when I was in the sixth grade. Roy worked for farmers as a laborer many years, then worked at a gas station. Edwin, their first son, was born March 2, 1949, while Richard Anthony, Margie Ree, Rose Marie, and Mary Jo were born in the next decade.

An excellent manager of the family's meager resources, her diligence kept her family well-fed and clothed during some difficult times. While raising her children, Dorcas worked in various clothes manufacturing plants. In addition to being an excellent seamstress, her hobbies were playing the guitar, singing, and working in the garden. Canning and preserving fruits and vegetables occupied a large portion of her time each spring and summer.

In hindsight, I probably should have reached out to Dot more during my teens and beyond. Her husband drank a lot on the weekends and I was afraid of him, even though he never bothered me. My family did not drink alcohol and was not very tolerant of his habit. She and the children visited our parents regularly, and I saw them fairly often.

The Fourth Brother

Ezra "Buzzie" Nathaniel Busbee was born on May 28, 1930, the first sibling with a May birthday. Growing to about five feet, eight inches tall and weighing about 160 to 165 pounds, he had a light complexion like our mother, blue eyes, and light brown hair, a change from blond hair at birth.

I remember Buzzie walking to Crossroad School with the younger children and dependably plowing the fields a lot while I was still young. Older brothers were either working in Columbia or in the military. On special occasions, he spent his hard-earned money on the younger siblings.

Buzzie's first job away from home was at a Spur Service Station on Main Street in Columbia around 1949–50. Along with other single young adults who were away from home, his boarding home landlord provided breakfast and the evening meal for him. Yet he came back home to Swansea often, and I remember running to meet him whenever his ride dropped him off. As younger kids, we wanted to see what he brought us. It may have been bubble gum or peppermint candy!

In the fall of 1951, Buzzie married Juanita Humphries. They lived for several years in an older home on Columbia's Olympia Avenue that was renovated to a duplex apartment. Later Buzzie and Juanita bought a house on White Avenue in West Columbia.

With a loving heart and a gentle spirit (like my mom), Buzzie was cool and level-headed regardless of the situation. His love and compassion were evident on a daily basis. Empty platitudes had no place in his life. Even though he was a male, it is easy to compare him with Martha and Mary in the scriptures. In that account, one sister chose the secular part of life, while the other chose the better walk within the spiritual realm. In the same way as the latter, "Buzzie" loved in a way that I may never know. He simply chose to be good.

Our relationship was close, especially in my upper teens and beyond. He was my friend as well as my brother, with similar emotional make-up. Whenever things troubled me, he always seemed to know. Sometimes it seemed as if he could read my mind, with an extra measure of perception. After talking to him, I always felt better.

After beginning my first full-time job with Southern Bell in Columbia, I lived with my siblings until I married in September 1961. For four of those years, I lived with Ezra and Juanita on White Avenue in West Columbia, South Carolina. We rode together to work in his "Cig Vendors" truck. These rides provided time for some very deep discussions. Although we did not agree on everything, we were never disagreeable. His soft heart forgave my youthful thinking.

Reflecting his compassion, Buzzie and Juanita took responsibility for Horace and Valarie's six-year-old son, Horace, Jr. when his parents' marriage broke up. It was a situation that left four children fatherless, and Ezra loved and nurtured Horace, Jr. for years.

His hobbies included playing his guitar and singing, often playing his guitar for little "Junior" (Horace, Jr.) to sing. He also liked to hunt for small game. For many years, he would work a garden, then freeze or can the produce himself. He devoted many, many hours each year to his church in various capacities.

Dorcas, Roy & Edwin

Horace in the Army
Around 1942

Horace as a cab driver

Horace in old age

Dorcas at about 20 yrs old

Dorcas in upper teens With her guitar

Chapter 4

David Jeremiah Busbee, Esther Mae Raines Williams (née Busbee), and Nellie Ruth Smith (née Busbee)

My Fifth Brother

David Jeremiah Busbee was my parent's sixth child, born as a very sickly child on May 16, 1932. Although each of Mom's babies was breast-fed, this nourishment was apparently insufficient to produce the desired growth in Jeremiah. It must have been a while before our parents recognized there was a genuine problem with this baby boy. After he was given goat's milk, his health began to change for the better.

No one is really sure what caused Jeremiah's stunted development. However, he was five years old before he could walk. I have little knowledge about his early developmental years, except for the awareness that doctors in that community lacked the training and/or experience that are available today. Most farm families struggled to eke out a living, much less being able to search out extensive medical care. This is not fault-finding, but rather a fact of life.

At the age of seven, Jeremiah started school and struggled academically from the onset. In the 1940s, children were held back until they grasped the subject matter. Many of the same teachers who taught him also taught me. We were in the same class by the time I was in the sixth grade even though he was five years older. Miss Dowling, our sixth-grade teacher was excellent, but extremely strict. Especially tough on lesson assignments, her goal was perfection in homework. It had to be redone until it was error-free, or the child would be spanked with a paddle. As a result, Jeremiah had his share. When I came to his rescue, I almost got into trouble with my helping him. When I left home, he was still in high school. After a number of years, he dropped out of school in the tenth grade.

Sometime during junior high school, it was discovered that Jeremiah's vision was very poor. Glasses were a real blessing, yet there continued to be a problem. School officials suggested transferring him to Cedar Springs School for blind and deaf children near Spartanburg, South Carolina. This suggestion was never heeded, and good intent fell by the wayside. He wore thick glasses for many years. However, his sight seemed to improve after cataract surgery.

Similar to his older siblings, Jeremiah had blue eyes and fair skin. When he should have been grown by the 1950s, he was still somewhat small, five feet, five or six inches, and about 150 pounds, but looked and acted like a child. His hobbies were riding a three-wheel bicycle and talking on the telephone endlessly. For a while, he planted a garden. He never learned to drive and became quite dependent on others. The siblings handled the situation as best they could.

At this point, I must interrupt this book's order to provide additional clarifying information. After our mother died in 1975, Jeremiah lived alone at the old home place. In the late 1970s, he developed serious breathing problems. Several doctors at Lexington County Medical Center, in conjunction with University of California - Berkeley discovered that his pituitary gland was not developed and placed Jeremiah on hormones. As a result, life was never the same. His voice changed and facial features matured overnight, as he grew taller and gained weight. In effect, Jeremiah became a man in body , yet remained a boy mentally. The rest is history for a future time.

My Second Sister

Esther Mae Raines Williams (née Busbee) was born at home in Lexington County, South Carolina, on April 20, 1934, our parents' second daughter and seventh child. During that period of time, many babies were delivered by a midwife in the home, as was the situation with Esther. She had lovely blue eyes and pretty blond hair, was about five feet, five inches tall and very slender, weighing about 125 pounds as an adult.

Around four or five years old, Esther became very ill and was diagnosed with acute influenza. In that time, discoveries of antibiotics and antiviral medications had not yet taken place. This illness was quite serious and lingered for a long time. As is often the case, children and young people with prolonged fevers develop rheumatic fever, a chronic inflammatory disease induced by a preceding infection. One of the numerous results is heart inflammation. No one seemed to know that Esther had damage to the valves in her heart. It was only after the fact that we became aware of it.

Three years older, Esther matured much faster than I. Much of my early information about the "facts of life" came from her rather than from Mom. She was full of vigor and liked to have fun and developed an early interest in boys. She was cute and developed by age fourteen, and boys were very interested in her. Although our parents did not let her date, it did not keep the guys from visiting her!

From my earliest memory, we shared a bed. With so many children, no one had much privacy and we shared everything. She was really active and a lot of fun.

One of my special memories of her was that she loved to fix my hair. I was her "guinea pig." After the Saturday night bath, she ripped up strips of paper or rags and curled my hair. The next morning she made corkscrew curls in my hair. Curls were popular back then. In hindsight, it lasted way too long because I think my final curls came in the seventh or eighth grade. I guess I thought the curls made me prettier or something.

School was not Esther's cup of tea. She certainly had the capability but not the interest or the motivation to excel. On one occasion, I helped her with a writing project. We almost got into big trouble, since we had the same English teacher and she recognized my writing style. I also remember helping her in spelling.

However, home economics suited her well. As a good seamstress and cook, these skills were helpful as she raised six children. In addition, she possessed great musical talent as a singer, and guitar and accordion player. Her talent was used while singing in church events, including one such event when she met her future husband.

At the ripe age of seventeen, Esther got married and moved to Gastonia, North Carolina. Her first child, Carolyn Ruth Raines, was born on February 12, 1952. When our family went to Gastonia to visit the new baby, I was a tenth grader marking the first time to travel outside South Carolina. Dad drove his old Hudson, jam-packed with children. Sometime between 1952 and June 1954, the Raines family moved back to Columbia.

Four of Esther's children, Carolyn, Debra, Georgia, and Joy, were born during the 1950s. Sons Edward and David were born in the 1960s. She did a good job making sure that the children were well fed and clothed. It is to her credit that all the children were educated, and many of them have a lot of musical talent.

My Turn

Born Nellie Ruth Busbee on October 31, 1936, I was their eighth child, after five brothers and two sisters.

For a couple who wanted two children, either something magical happened or they made a lot of mistakes. Seriously, I would rather believe that children are gifts from God, since Jeremiah 1:5 states that God knew me in my mother's womb. There is power in that!

Like later siblings Lois and Hosea (Tracy), I was born at home in the southern tip of Lexington County, South Carolina, near Swansea. As a child, I had dark hair and hazel eyes (like my grandfather Aaron Busbee). This may not seem to be significant, except that all the other brothers and sisters were blonde and blue-eyed. People would often remark about my being different. Yet as a child, I could not comprehend why folks made comparisons. Sometimes I felt that having an olive complexion, brown eyes, and brown hair must be bad trademarks.

Once a man was visiting my dad and remarked about the pretty little girls. During the conversation, he said he would like to take me home with him. Due to my shyness, it frightened me so much that I hid under my parents' bed until he was gone. Being different caused me to be extremely shy, especially around strangers.

It seems that I matured slower than the other girls. I remember weighing sixty-five pounds in the seventh grade. Three years later, I was five feet, three inches tall and weighed 110 pounds. I gained no more than five pounds until the middle-age spread began in my forties, at which time I weighed 123 pounds for many years...at least until I retired from BellSouth!

At the age of fifteen, I landed my first job at Dodd's Five and Ten Cent Store, on State Street in West Columbia. The pay wasn't much for part-time Friday and Saturday work, but I managed well enough to cover school expenses, plus extra spending money. During one time period, I worked full-time at Dodd's while I tried to get a full scholarship to the University of South Carolina.

In January 1955, I accepted an accounting position at Southern Bell Telephone Company. After extensive testing, the manager told me that my math score was the highest ever achieved to that point. I am one of the very few employees who could get excited about a tax report, but I loved my work. It seemed as if I flowed with it, and earned a $39 gross weekly salary, too!

It may not seem like much, but earning $39 each week was so much more than that to which I had been accustomed. My first priority was making sure that Lois and Hosea had nice clothes while helping to meet their school needs. As mentioned previously, the very first big purchase was a washing machine for my mother. She began having some health issues soon thereafter, and it would have been quite difficult for Lois to go to school, work at home, and work outside the home. The job also provided opportunities to buy clothing for some nieces and nephews who were not as fortunate. It brought me so much joy to help my struggling family members.

By age seventeen, I became more interested in boys. At first, I went out with boys I had known for some years, before broadening my scope.

Edna watched carefully and monitored my choices. She may have been stricter than my parents, since they didn't always get to meet the guys.

The next year, I met a special young man who held my fancy for four years. I talked about him so much that Lois must have thought I had morphed into someone else. She was a good listener and endured many ups-and-downs with me. One challenge was that our maturity levels were not anywhere near the same. He had been in the military and experienced life on a much broader scope. He thought that I was tied to my parents' apron strings, but that was not the case. I simply wanted an easier life for my younger siblings and was determined to make it happen. Through life experiences, I've realized that only our Creator understands the innermost parts of our being. By the way, both Lois and Hosea got married before that decade ended and I was still single. The best was yet to come, I met my future husband on June 10, 1959!

I have enjoyed various hobbies, especially reading, traveling, sewing, canning/freezing, and decorating. Over the years, I have received many ribbons for canning/pickling and sewing in the State Fair and the Bell System Telephone Pioneers.

As noted earlier, an area for which the Busbee Family was noted related to its musical ability. Eight of the ten children played at least one instrument, but Jeremiah and I could not play anything except the radio or canned music. However, I rated first place in Telephone Pioneer Convention for my writing a series of Bible School lessons on love and marriage for teenagers. I tend to think of myself as energetic, compassionate, and sentimental. A young pastor once described me as "light and lively."

Perhaps the best summary is my philosophy of life: "Give of my love and services freely, knowing that greater things will be returned to me."

Jeremiah at 15
1947-48

Jeremiah at 17
1949-50

Jeremiah about 20

Ruth in 7th
1948-49

Ruth

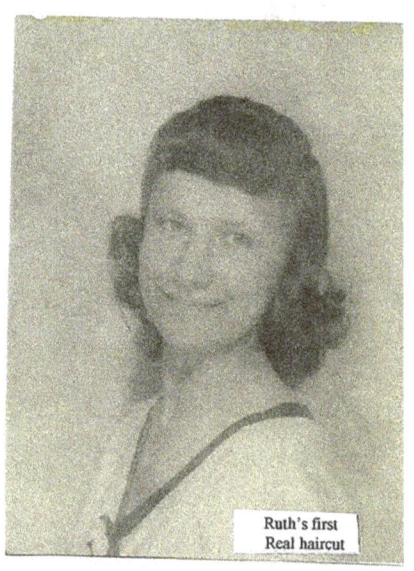
Ruth's first Real haircut

Chapter 5

Lois Crosia Moore (née Busbee) and Hosea Andrew "Tracy" Busbee

Lois Crosia Moore - My Youngest Sister

Lois Crosia Moore was our parents' youngest daughter. A cute little girl, Lois was born October 29, 1938, and became a lovely teenager with pretty blue eyes, long blond hair, and fair skin like our mother. In fact, her hair was never short until after her marriage. My future husband, O. J. Smith, cut off at least a foot of her hair in 1959 and it was still shoulder length!

Our lives were interwoven from her birth until her death at sixty-three years old. Although quiet like Mama, Lois was stubborn and never wanted to say she could be wrong. In all probability she may have been smarter than I. She never seemed to study as much, yet we had the same class ranking at our graduations.

As children and early teens, we traded clothes and shoes all the time. People thought we had more clothes that way. Once she hit puberty, though, it was "bye-bye" to trading. She was about three inches taller and twenty to thirty pounds heavier. She weighed between 140 pounds to 145 pounds. Exchanging shoes also became impossible, since her feet kept growing until her shoes were larger. While it lasted, trading was fun and useful. I remember particularly our "Sunday best"—my pair of blue slippers and her pair of the same shoe in a different color. We also had one pair of school shoes each. In my later years in high school, I shared a bed with her. We took turns getting up and starting a fire in the living room fireplace, then we started breakfast. She became annoyed with me when I would ask her to get up. Early on, she liked to cook more than I did. Cooking was her cup of tea. She seemed to live to cook, while I cooked to live.

As little girls, we did just about everything together and had so much in common that our dad would sometimes call one of us by the other's name. We played the same games, swam, and had the same make-believe friends. Even in grade school, we hung close and shared some of the same friends. It always made her happy when someone gave us matching things. Only once did we get into a squabble. That's when I thought I could teach her a thing or two about one of her weaker areas—directions. Our dad settled that dispute quickly by reading us some scriptures and warned us never to argue. That settled it!

During high school, Lois's workload at home was heavy due to Mom's illnesses. I was already working at Southern Bell in Columbia, but I went back to Swansea most weekends to help as much as possible. Because she helped so much at home, I paid all of her school expenses and the cost of her senior trip.

Our bond was always strong, but our personalities were very different. She was an introvert and very private. Most things were big secrets. Even though I knew she appreciated everything that was done for her, she never showed much emotion. On the other end of the scale, almost anyone could " read" my facial expressions that could not hide my joy whenever anything special was done for me.

Lois played the piano and led singing in her church for years. Her hobbies were cooking and sewing, with a lot of clothes and items made for her home.

In November of 1957, she met her future husband, Luther Moore. On a double date with them, my friend told me that they were going to get married. I thought he had lost his mind! Yet he was right, and plans were being made. Lois and Luther married without telling our parents on January 24, 1958. Her first son, Sammy, was born in December 1958, and Michael was born in October 1959. Their daughter Sandra was born in May 1966.

I was always grateful for a sister like Lois, and I loved her very much.

My youngest brother

The tenth and final sibling, Hosea Andrew "Tracy" Busbee, was born November 23, 1941, two weeks before Japan bombed Pearl Harbor. It was fortunate that our oldest brother had already established his family, since there was little room for a new baby!

From the very beginning, he was definitely a little man. I remember telling our mother that he had a fuzzy face, and this little tyke became my pride and joy. Although he was another cotton-top, he looked a lot like me and that made me feel good about myself. His eyes were blue, and he had a light olive complexion and blond hair that became darker later in life. As an adult, he was six feet, two inches tall and weighed about 170 pounds. He always carried himself well and looked slender, trim, and fit.

This little fellow learned at an early age how to get his way. Whenever he would get into trouble with our parents, he always pretended to get sleepy, while "on the red carpet." It was difficult to see him get a spanking, but he deserved a lot of them.

During that season of life, young boys wore short pants or long shirts that looked somewhat like a dress. By age two, Tracy had never owned overalls or long denim pants, and Edna went shopping and bought "big boy" clothes for him. In his excitement to show our dad his new clothes, Tracy took off running. Apparently, he forgot the back doorsteps, and his inertia kept him running forward. When he hit the ground, the large bone (tibia) in his right leg was badly broken. Moore's Clinic set his leg and we carried him around for a couple of months. It seems difficult to believe, but he is the only sibling who ever broke a bone in our family. With our climbing trees and jumping out of the hay loft, that is a miracle!

From an early age, Tracy did a lot of plowing in the fields and worked hard at whatever he was assigned to do. He learned quickly to perform well. Together we picked cotton, peas, corn, and anything else that needed to be reaped. He never seemed to mind and didn't complain.

After I went to work at Southern Bell, I liked to take him shopping in Columbia. We would pick some nice dress clothes with vibrant colors. He was so handsome in a pink shirt and navy pants! The one thing that I remember most was his deep appreciation for anything. It was such a wonderful feeling just seeing his smiling face…. a grin that wouldn't go away. He was an adorable teenager.

On numerous occasions when I did not have a way back to Columbia on the weekend, he would walk with me to downtown Swansea to catch a Greyhound bus. His long legs went much faster than was normal for me, but we made it. He had a caring heart and a loving spirit. A niece told me one day that she would have known that he was my brother, even if no one ever told her. She said we were built the same emotionally. That is not at all bad!

Tracy's hobbies include a variety of sports, fishing, hunting, and camping. He also learned to play the guitar at a young age and did it well. When young he taught me how to be tough, climbing trees and jumping from the barn loft into the load of hay on the wagon. I treasure our relationship and take pride in saying that he is my "little brother."

Lois, Ruth & Ruby Fallaw

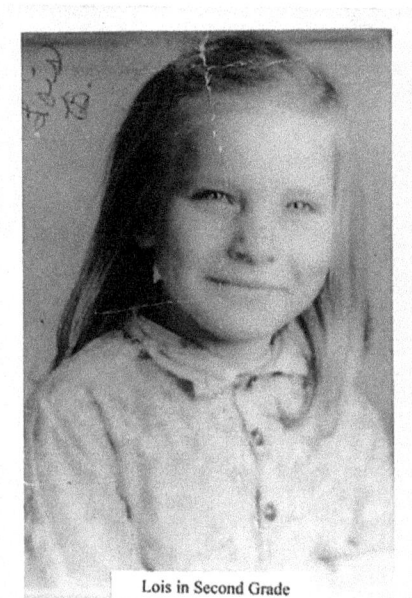

Lois in Second Grade

Lois as a High School Senior

Lois and her son Sammy

Lois as a bride & Ruth

Hosea
At 3 Yrs.

Hosea
2nd grade

Hosea
at 14-15

Hosea
about 12

Hosea
17yrs old

PART 2

EDUCATION AND FUN

Chapter 6

Educational Opportunities

Let's Go to School!

I was called a "bookworm," and it started early. When my oldest sister Dorcas took me with her to school for the first time, I was probably three or four years old. The reason is unknown, but I became a five-year-old scholastic veteran when starting to attend the small country "Cross Roads School."

The wood-paneled school was approximately three miles from home. We walked most of the time, although sometimes we would get a ride at least part of the way.

My first-grade teacher, Mrs. Maude Shumpert, planted a desire for knowledge within me. With loving guidance, she became a treasured, unique teacher. Mrs. Shumpert also played a significant role in my future penmanship. Taking pencils repeatedly from my left hand and placing them in the right hand, she simply would not let me be a lefty. I remained with her through the third grade, after which I had Miss Myrtie Martin, who taught fourth through seventh grades. These ladies opened up a new world to me, allowing reading of any desired books.

I recall one significant lesson when I was in the second or third grade. After taking off my shoes at school when it turned warm on a fall day, I didn't consider how cold it would become that night. What a wakeup call I had the next morning when I had to walk to school barefoot! The experience taught me a valuable lesson.

In this tiny school, there was a real lunchroom where children received their plates and ate at their desks. It was here that I experienced my first store-bought bread. A dear old lady prepared a good meal and washed all the dishes for the whole school, which included about thirty people. I would take my loaf bread home to Lois.

This school was a wooden building painted white with a tin roof. Since it had outdoor bathrooms, I am not at all sure about the water system in the lunchroom. The heating system consisted of two pot-bellied wood- or coal-burning stoves. Our desks were traditional wood with metal frames and had ink wells and slots for pencils.

At the end of the fourth grade, we were told that we would transfer to schools in the little town of Swansea. This was a shocking development, with three-hundred grade school children instead of thirty. Despite the adjustments, my early training in good work habits paid off and I was soon at the top of the class with good grades. After all, whenever Mr. Roy Whitaker came by driving the big yellow bus, it was so much better than the long walk!

Looking back, I wonder why I felt so overwhelmed at the number of kids in our school, since I knew each of them by name before I realized it.

Red-haired and newly married, Mrs. Thelma Williams taught me in fifth grade. Sometimes she would ask me to assist a slower-paced child. I also remember most that Mrs. Williams and Lois's second grade teacher, Mrs. Rast, would ask us to spell words for them during recess. "Cross Roads" must have prepared us for that!

Miss Hazel Dowling was an excellent sixth grade teacher, but extremely strict. Any homework errors had to be redone until perfected. When homework was not corrected and turned in quickly, the student would get a spanking with a paddle. Despite the tough discipline, Miss Dowling had a tender heart for the children who struggled academically. When my brother Jeremiah was challenged as a slow learner, she visited our home to learn about the functioning of our family through the eyes of a "city girl."

Grade-school years passed swiftly, and junior high was in the same two-story brick-veneered building as the elementary grades. Both floors had a wide hall traversing the center of the building, with stairwells at the end of each hall. Restrooms were on both sides of the hall at each end, with real sinks and toilets, but no partitions.

We did not change classes in the seventh or eighth grade. Whenever a change was necessary, the teachers changed classrooms. I cannot remember the name of my seventh-grade teacher, but Mrs. McCormick from North taught eighth grade. I recall that I was small for a twelve-year-old.

My first nighttime school party was in eighth grade at the log-built Community House, south of Swansea and built by the WPA during the Great Depression. My brother Ezra escorted me that night.

By age thirteen, it was time to attend Swansea High School, a facility opened in 1927 that faced Lawrence Avenue. A dirt street separated it from the Swansea Elementary school, which faced that same street. The high school was constructed somewhat like the grade school but was much more modern. The school cafeteria was in a separate but nearby block building, with long dining tables and folding chairs.

I loved school and, as noted earlier, books were "my cup of tea." Math and English were my favorite subjects. I did well in all subjects and had an intense desire to do well. At home, I studied when everyone else had long since gone to bed. Many times, Dad made me go to bed against my wishes, but he knew that 6 a.m. came early.

I changed classes for the first time in ninth grade, when we were allowed to pick some of our subjects while others were picked for us. From day one, I liked algebra.

My American history class was taught by our football coach, Mr. Robert Sanders, who frequently assigned special projects to me. I remember when he told the class, "If you want someone to carry out a project, you need to ask a busy person."

I nearly got into real trouble once, because I helped my older sister Esther write her term paper. Unfortunately, we had the same English teacher. I hadn't written her entire paper, I had just helped a bit, but the teacher recognized my style and questioned Esther about it intently. Somehow, we got off the hook.

Mrs. Agnes Cope was my homeroom and home economics instructor in the ninth grade. She taught me many life skills, which included sewing, crocheting, meal planning, and cooking.

Most of the girls who took home economics were also in the FHA (Future Homemakers Association) club. Most of the boys took agriculture or shop and belonged to the FFA club (Future Farmers Association). One benefit came when members went to the camp at Myrtle Beach. I also joined the 4-H Club that year.

The classes were very similar in tenth grade to ninth grade, except Mrs. Jimmie Rast was homeroom teacher. This was my introduction to typing classes, using old manual Remington typewriters. Mrs. Rast made sure that everyone understood the keyboard. By the end of the second year, I could type sixty-five words per minute, considered above-average on the older typewriters.

Involvement continued with the FHA and 4-H clubs. 4-H Club members worked on certain projects, financial planning, clothing, home furnishings, and house planning, where I actually drew a plan for my dream home. While in Miss Halbert's tenth-grade English class, ninth-grader Perry Wendell Neese placed a hairpin in the radiator used for heating and played a tune with it. His mischief disturbed the teacher so much that she stopped the lesson and stated, "Wendell, I am your teacher!"(As an adult, Perry worked hard and became a Colonel in the National Guard and retired as a General.)

I was inducted that year into the National Beta Club, which required an "A" average. As our sponsor, Mrs. Marie Rast (C.L.) liked to take us to Orangeburg's Edisto Gardens on the Edisto River. We would take a picnic lunch and spend the day.

The work pace really picked up in my junior year. Although our family had a busy schedule and school, I still managed to help in the fund-raising campaigns for the Junior-Senior Banquet and our senior trip to Washington, D.C. We sold everything from candy to magazine subscriptions. Since the school was composed of middle-class and poor children, we had to work really hard to obtain enough money for any project. I won my first watch for extra effort as the top salesperson.

As a junior, I was not very interested in dating yet. I turned down everyone that invited me to be his guest at the Junior-Senior Banquet. For that special occasion, I borrowed a baby blue evening gown to wear with my ballerina shoes and went alone. My older brother Floyd and wife Edna drove me to the banquet. He thought that his little country sister was so beautiful that he cried.

During my senior year, we sponsored a baby contest. My neighbor, Dale Hutto, was a beautiful four-year-old when I sponsored her. I can't remember who won.

When I was a senior, the director of the Vocational Division of Curtis Publishing Company wrote to commend me for a grand job in the magazine subscription campaign. He stated that more than three million students participated in selling and that only one out of a hundred achieved the record that I set. *Sand Hill Script*, our school newspaper, offered these congratulations and good wishes as follows: "Ruth is a senior who not only works at her lessons but who also works at her home and outside her home. She does a good share of the housework, holds down a job in Columbia on Friday afternoons and Saturdays, and continues to make a grade of "A" on every school subject. Not many people can equal her record."

During that year, the faculty and student body selected me as their representative for the Daughters of the American Revolution "Good Citizenship" award. It was based upon dependability, service, leadership, loyalty, and patriotism. These qualities include truthfulness, punctuality, consideration of others, ability to assume responsibility, and an unselfish interest in family, school, community, and nation. I had received many Beta Club, 4-H Club, and FHA certificates and served on the *Swansean* annual staff during my senior year, but no recognition meant as much to me as being selected the "Good Citizen." This was truly a high honor to be selected from among a number of worthy students.

It seems hard to believe now, but I had my first real date my senior year for the Junior-Senior Banquet. Jerry Branham, my date was a brother to one of my classmates. Tragically, he was killed in an auto accident during the summer after my graduation.

The finale of my high school days was in giving the salutatory address. All of my family was there and proud of me. Although the dream was to advance to college and become a teacher, my family could not afford it. The financial options available for today's youth did not exist then, or at least I did not know where to find help. I attempted to earn a scholarship to the University of South Carolina, but to no avail. Some years later I was accepted to USC through an entrance examination but enrolled at night due to work responsibilities.

Flash into the future…dreams did come true forty years later. While working full-time for Bell South in Columbia, I went back to collegiate night classes in September 1990 and graduated with a Bachelors in Business Administration from Southern Wesleyan University (magna cum laude) in December 1994. During the summer of 2005, the South Carolina Department of Education certified me as a teacher in Accounting, Business, and Computer Science. That certification is comical, since my knowledge of computers far exceeds any practical experience.

Cross Road School as it appeared in the 1940's.
It was situated on W. E. Jeffcoat Road near Sharon Church Road.
Picture belongs to Mrs. Barbara Hutto Poole and used by permission.

Swansea Grammer School on Lawrence Avenue in Swansea, S. C.
This building was torn down around 1953 to make room for gym.
Picture belongs to Mrs. Barbara Hutto Poole and used by permission.

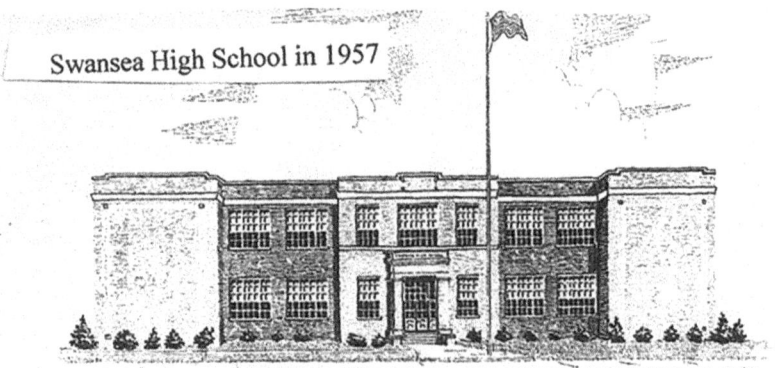

Swansea High School in 1957

THE NATIONAL SOCIETY OF THE
Daughters of the American Revolution

THIS CERTIFIES THAT Ruth Busbee having been selected as the GOOD CITIZEN of the Swansea High School for the current year, through her demonstration during her entire course of the qualities of Dependability, Leadership, Service and Patriotism, is hereby awarded this D. A. R. GOOD CITIZENS CERTIFICATE

Signed and awarded this thirty-first day of May 1954

Gertrude S. Carraway, PRESIDENT GENERAL N. S. D. A. R.

Jessamine Bland James, NATIONAL CHAIRMAN D. A. R. GOOD CITIZENS COMMITTEE

Mrs. James T. Queen Sr., STATE REGENT

D. A. R.

PRINCIPAL OF HIGH SCHOOL

Citizenship Candidate

Clipping from *The State*

Miss Ruth Busbee is Swansea High School's candidate for the DAR Good Citizenship Award. Miss Busbee was chosen for her qualities of dependability, truthfulness, punctuality, loyalty, and interest in everything worth while. She is the daughter of Mr. and Mrs. Andrew J. Busbee, of Swansea, and is an all-A student in the high school. She is a member of the twelfth grade.

The *Swansean* annual staff during my senior year.

Seated left to right are: Mary Lee Jumper, Frances Cook, Margaret Mather Sandra Flake, Howard Miller, Corinne Durham, and Mervelle Senn. Standing are Faye Yon, Billy Sturkie, De Lois Neese, Donald Berry, Ronnie Simmons, Sue Simmons, Francis Carroll Kennerly, Patty Amonds, Carol Heyward, and Ruth Busbee

All dressed up for my Junior Prom

Chapter 7

Fun and Play

Nothing beats the innocence of children. As siblings in a large, traditional farm family, we were a close-knit bunch. Since there was little extra money for toys, we learned to create our own playthings and used our imagination to come up with new games.

We built a playhouse in the woods, with all kinds of objects for furniture and dishes. We took turns being parents, and our food consisted of mud pies and various weeds, seeds, and roots for vegetables.

Our telephone system consisted of tin cans held together with a long string. Little did I know that I would spend forty-one years working for the "real" telephone company (BellSouth). Our simple telephone system worked well, since we could speak loud enough without our mouthpieces.

Some of my fondest memories revolve around Bull Swamp Creek. When summer became unbearably hot, without air conditioners or electric fans, we went swimming in the creek's icy water. It was in the dug-out swimming hole that I first learned to swim. Watermelons were placed in the running stream to cool while we swam and played. When we tired of playing, the watermelons were burst open. Inside the green rind was juicy red or yellow fruit that was so refreshing. Occasionally, we would cook out on the banks of the stream. The dense shade was much cooler than at home. The neighborhood girls, Ruby Fallaw and Myrtis Whitaker, would sometimes go swimming with the Busbee girls. Occasionally, we scrambled onto the creek bank when a snake would float by, waiting as it floated down the stream.

Horseback riding was also a fun thing. Dad's horses, Dolly and Lottie, were my favorites mares—just like family. Usually, we rode bareback unless Daddy rode with us. Dolly and Lottie would run to Dad, because they knew that he would give them a treat, usually an apple or watermelon when he called them from the pasture.

Horses require a lot of work. They needed to be curried or brushed each day and their stables needed to be kept clean of poo. They also eat quite a bit of corn, hay, and grain. I will write more about the horses' watering and stables in a later chapter.

Lois and I spent endless hours playing ball and jacks, a game that was very popular in the mid-to-late 1940s. It was simple but required skill to throw the small rubber ball up in the air and pick up the jacks before the ball hit the floor. Our neighbor, Ruby Fallaw, came to our house as early as 7 a.m. on Sundays, just to play jacks with us. Our grade school allowed us to play it on the sidewalks during recess.

As I recall, it seemed like the girls jumped rope and the boys played marbles much of the time. Jump rope was a great exercise game. Often when three or more of us had some spare time, two children would turn a long rope, which may have been used around the barnyard, while another would jump it. We would sing short tunes or rhymes to keep pace with the jumper, whose time was up at the end of the tune. Another child would jump to a new tune. It could go on for hours.

Anytime we had enough players in our age group, we loved to play Ring-Around-A-Rosy. Joining hands to form a circle, we moved to our left and sang:

Ring-around-a-rosy
A pocket full of posies;
Ashes, ashes
We all fall down!

    At the end of the song, we would stop quickly and everybody fell down. The last player down left the game. This continued until only one player, the winner, was left in the circle.

    My brothers liked to play marbles and sometimes they would play for keeps. The older boys would buy a "bum," an oversized marble. The "bum" seemed to be the prized possession. Anyone who owned a bum seemed to have special status. Our boys were no different from the men who needed their status.

    During the summer months, our farm seemed to *manufacture* June bugs. They are called this because they appear on June 1. We would catch them and tie a string around their legs, then make them fly. Now I understand that we were somewhat cruel to handle the little creatures just for fun but seeing the light on their bodies was a real thrill for the little ones.

    A June bug is actually a large beetle related to the ancient and sacred scarab beetle from Egypt. They are seen normally at night when light attracts them. They eat the young leaves of trees and shrubs. The adult beetle deposits its eggs in the ground of meadows, gardens, and fields. The larvae are large white grubs with brown heads and burrow into the soil in autumn and stay for two years. While in the ground, they feed on roots of corn, grains, and vegetables before coming out in May or June as adult beetles. As children, we would not have thought they were so much fun had we known that they ate our dad's crops. What a price!

    Floyd and Papa made a swing from an old tire with the middle portion cut out to leave a flat seating surface. Long ropes or chains were placed inside the hulled-out tire and hung upon a tall tree limb. Lois, Tracy, and I spent a lot of time swinging in the breeze. It was extraordinary when we learned to swing standing up. Real freedom!

Climbing trees was a great adventure. Ezra and Tracy taught me how. At first it was a little scary, but it became pure joy as I gained more experience. Our property had some trees called Poplars, with blossoms that looked a lot like the tulip tree. I found them very enticing. Scurrying up the limbs to fetch the blossoms caused me to risk a dangerous fall. My childhood bravery was somewhat foolish, but Mama always seemed to be thankful for the bouquets. She never scolded me or explained that I could have gotten badly hurt.

Although we never had stilts like some of our friends, we reverted to homemade versions made from tall tin cans smashed in the center to fit around the soles of our shoes. Long pieces of cord were threaded through holes we punched in the tops of the cans. We could actually walk on them and learned to balance ourselves.

Hopscotch was lots of fun when we had enough friends to make it lively and fast-moving. In this game, a player tossed a small stone into one square after another that had been drawn on the ground, hopping from section to section to pick up the stone after each toss. This game was really good exercise and required a lot of stamina.

In the back, our house sat high off the ground. During rainy weather, Lois and I liked to play under the house in the dry sand where small creatures lived that we called "doodle bugs." These insects made funnel-shaped holes in the dry soil. One of us would get a straw, toothpick, or tiny twig, stir the sand at the bottom of hole and recite these words:

"Doodle Bug, Doodle Bug, Fly away home,
Your house is on fire and the children are alone,

All except one who is named Anne,
And she is hid under the frying pan."

Sure enough, in a short time the little creature would appear at the bottom of his funnel hole. This pea-sized bug would then curl up into a ball and appear to be dead. When we were not playing under the house, we were playing in mud puddles and walking in the rain. It was great fun since all of the Busbee children went barefoot in the summer, except for Sunday church.

My brothers enjoyed their slingshots, homemade from a forked stick found on the family farm. The rubber came from old discarded inner tubes and a strip of leather found in a barn or stable. Most of the boys were good at their aim with nice stones picked up from the field or barnyard. Our young males were quite creative with their designs.

The younger children really enjoyed bubbles. If we were fortunate enough to have a bubble pipe, we were " in hog heaven" and moved up a notch on the exclusive club. Playing with a bubble pipe could last for hours.

Another special pastime was my paper dolls. My sisters were not as interested in them as I, but that didn't matter. In those times, it was rare for any children to act bored, as can happen with children today.

PART 3

My Home and Hometown

Chapter 8

The House and Surroundings

The Good Old Days

The following is an essay written for my English #1054 class while attending Southern Wesleyan University (Columbia Campus) under Dr. Lindsay Hislop. It is a Comparison & Contrast Essay written by me (Ruth B. Smith) on March 14, 1991.

People speak of the "good old days"; I have come to realize that those days were not necessarily good. Growing up in the country in a home without modern conveniences and furnishings, with all its sentimental attachments, was not as pleasant as living in my modern home.

My parents' wood house that was built at the turn of the century posed a potential problem of being a fire hazard; whereas my house constructed of brick with a fire alarm system should be safer. Our house has brick steps with wrought iron railings instead of wooden steps without a hand rail. We could hear every drop of rain on the tin roof as it fell pitter-patter; now we can barely hear the sound of rain on the asphalt shingles.

Heating with a fireplace and stove may have been acceptable in Dad's day, but thermostatic controls in each room have their benefits. We never really adjusted to the cold hard floors in the harsh winters; sliding our feet off the bed onto warm wall-to-wall carpet does not jolt the nervous system. Going to the outdoor privy with two holes for seats at night could get scary, so our colored bathroom fixtures have been a Godsend. Most people do not consider the value of running water at the turn of a knob unless there has been an experience of getting water from a manual pump using force. One tiny light hung from the ceiling in each room in Dad's house; on the other hand we have a different type fixture in each room in the Smith house.

Manicured grass has replaced the sandy yards that were kept clean by sweeping. Mom's colorful flower garden full of annuals has its counterpart in azaleas and dogwoods with some tulips and daffodils. The umbrella-like chinaberry tree shaded an outdoor table we often used to eat on; in its place the newer home has patio furniture on a cement patio with surrounding pines.

Entertainment with no telephone, no television, and one large radio setting in the living room caused the large family to intermingle. The added features of four telephones, four televisions, several radios and a stereo are fine, but I miss the interaction with family. The hot summers would have been unbearable without the swimming hole at the creek, but our house has its own built-in swimming pool. Eating at a long table covered with oilcloth that had benches on each side to seat twelve people has been replaced with the modern round version seating four people. Even though there are sentimental memories of the "good old days," I wish to remain in the modern times.

My Dad's House

My parents lived somewhere else in the earliest years of their marriage, but the house where I was born and raised was built around 1900, more or less. No one is absolutely certain when construction was completed.

The Busbee property was inherited from my dad's maternal grandfather, Samuel Harsey. Apparently, my great-grandfather deeded the property to my grandmother Nancy E. Busbee and her son (Uncle) Haskell Harsey (who was born prior to her marriage to Aaron Busbee), before my dad's birth in September 1892. The deed remained until Dad purchased Uncle Haskell's rights on December 22, 1941, with eighty-six acres in the home place and thirty in the upper place. The family's oral history shows that the Harsey family owned hundreds of acres of land, which were handed down to Samuel Harsey's eight children.

The original house was built with unpainted lumber and the sills sat on stone piers. Boards were nailed in a perpendicular pattern (cross-wise) rather than vertically, and the inside walls were also wooden. There was no underpinning and the backside of the house sat high off the ground. As noted earlier, I spent many rainy days playing under it as a child.

The floors were finished boards that my parents covered with various pieces of linoleum, many of which were colorful. Front and back steps were also wooden, with no handrails or added supports. At the top of the back steps was a stand that held a wash basin and towel where anyone coming in from the fields could clean up before entering the kitchen area.

The roof was made of tin and designed somewhat like today's gabled roofs, with the highest point behind the stone chimney on the south side of the house and northward to a point over a bedroom window. The kitchen portion of the roof went under the lowest side of the other roof line, also tin. Since tin rusts after years of use, ours had evidence of discoloration. The stone chimney was fairly wide at ground level, probably six or seven feet. As the chimney went upward, it became smaller—no more than three feet at the apex.

The most cherished piece of furniture was Dad's upright organ. High above the keyboard was an extension that had a mirror and two wide cubicles with pictures and keepsakes. The organ had pedals that were pumped to make music. Our home had an abundance of musical instruments; eight of the ten children played one or more of them and we sang together often. Our only radio sat in the corner near the organ. An old dresser was against the wall opposite the fireplace. It was on this dresser that the men brought a wash basin with hot water to shave. It could be a busy spot with so many guys in the house! I think that Dad used a straight razor, but my memory is somewhat unclear about that.

Seating the big family was accomplished with several wooden rockers and many straight-back wood chairs. The room bore no semblance of luxury. People sometimes sat on a daybed in the room, but someone slept on it at night. The wall behind this bed had many family pictures. Some were quite old and passed down from my grandparents.

Iron-framed double beds were placed throughout the house, all with ticks and thick mattresses. Ticks were heavy cloth cases made like mattresses but filled with wheat or oat straw. These were used in lieu of box springs and were very common in this time. There were a few feather mattresses, and an abundance of hand-stitched quilts, mostly made by my aunt, Gertrude Sightler. The fancier ones may have been handed down from an older generation, a farming family tradition. At least two of us slept in each bed, and it was only after I left home in 1955 that I had a bed to myself. That was an adjustment with still no heat in my bedroom at night. I got cold feet, until I bought an electric blanket. Whenever we had overnight guests, we children slept on a pallet on the living room floor. The pallet was made of quilts and spare pillows placed on the bare floor.

Storage was sparse. Large, heavy trunks were everywhere for clothes and any other valuables. Long rods held clothes that needed to be hung, and sheets covered the hanging clothes to keep off dust. Each child had his/her own assigned space on a big book cabinet. Throughout the house, every empty space was filled with canned fruit and vegetables, harvested and preserved for the winter. Every shelf and much of the space under the many beds were used as storage space.

Floors were swept with brooms of "broom straw" grass, then mopped with rag mops and/or scrubbed with a brush. Flour and feed sacks became dish and dust cloths. We used whatever was available. Other aspects of the house are described in other chapters.

Outside Surroundings

About a hundred feet from the back of the house, in a semicircle of sort, were a corn crib, the big barn with a hay loft, and a row of horse stables with a wooden-fenced enclosure protruding out front.

The corn crib was square, built from logs, and had a tin roof. The barn was one of my favorite places to play. My brothers and I had great fun jumping from the second story loft into a wagon load of hay or grain. It is a miracle no one ever broke a leg or arm.

Each backyard structure had a tin roof, and the area had three or four large, old oak trees. The chicken house was closer to the house, under some very large and old chinaberry trees. Under the trees was a long table that had many purposes described elsewhere in this book. Cow stalls and pigpens were about two hundred yards from the house and other buildings, near another log barn and placed some distance away because of the hog and cow manure stench. All of the animals' body waste (manure) was used as fertilizer and hauled to a field and spread over it with pitchforks and/or shovels.

Near the front of the house were a number of gardenias; the blossoms were sweet smelling and pretty. At the south and north side of the house were many cannas of various colors. They were bright orange, rust, yellow, red, and pink. Their blossoms started in early spring and lasted until the frost killed them in October. The bushes had large leaves; some were dark green, while others were variegated. These flowers made pretty floral arrangements for the house or to share with others. The tubers were left in the ground and came up every year.

Close to the house were purple, red, and yellow four-o-clocks. The four-o-clock is an annual and will come up from the seeds left on the ground. They have an unusual characteristic in that the bloom is tight most all day but opens up in the late afternoon.

Several large cedars were between the house and the driveway.

A semicircle driveway was in front of the house coming off Jones Wire Road. The area in front of the house was quite large. It was at least a half-acre. This area had many different flowering plants and, at times, some garden grown vegetables, including peas or beans. The flower garden was a family project. We planted many annuals marigolds, zinnias, black-eyed Susans, and nasturtiums. Marigolds are supposed to keep insects away; the others are for their beauty. One of Mom's favorite flowers was bachelor button. We sometimes planted what we called cockscomb (celosia). The road embankment was covered with running roses. They were pink or red. We children really enjoyed the roses.

A lot of time was spent in the flower garden. Each person had a favorite. My brother Ezra really liked nasturtiums and took great care to find new varieties of seeds to plant and cultivate. Our mother liked a variety of bachelor buttons. Some preferred verbena or poppies.

Our woods were full of dogwoods, crabapple, jasmine, and honeysuckles. In the month of May, I liked to pick pink mountain laurels for teachers and friends. In the summer I would climb the poplar trees for their tulip-like blossoms for my mother, never thinking that I could fall. We were not a bored bunch of kids but created our own fun.

The "wood pile" was on the north side of the house where the grown men in the family piled logs and large branches to be cut into pieces for the fireplace and the kitchen stove. The men used a crosscut saw to get the trees or limbs on the ground. Two adults operated the saw with one on each end of the saw while holding a handle and pulling it.

Sometimes smaller trees or limbs were cut with a wood axe by one person. Once the logs were brought home and piled, the younger kids cut them into pieces for use. We all worked to keep the area neat and clean.

A drastic change came in the way yards are managed. Back in the olden days, it was not at all uncommon to have sandy yards instead of lawns. We had no grass in the yards. I suppose it may have derived from the fact that a farmer fought grass in his fields. Our yard was very large with front and back areas. Any debris was swept away with a broom made from brush shrubs. We literally would sweep the dirt, just like we did with the kitchen floor, except with a different type of broom. The yard broom was much heavier and cruder. Whenever guest were expected, we spent days making sure the yards were clean and free of any trash.

Animals that Lived in Our Surroundings

There was diversity, to say the least, in the critters that dwelled within a stone's throw of our living quarters. It is somewhat hard to declare which ones were more important. Since it would have been impossible to farm manually without our horses, let's begin with them. Two or more horses always lived on the farm during the years that I lived with my parents.

The ones I loved and remember most were Dolly and Lottie. Both were roan-colored horses. Both were very large mares. At several points in time, we had a male horse. These animals seemed almost like family. They would eat from our hands and liked fruit and watermelon just like us children. Sometimes we had mules. A great deal of time and money were spent growing food such as corn, oats, and hay for them. They had to be groomed every day to keep their beautiful appearance. A couple times in my life, I have been told that I "was as stubborn as a mule."

Dogs were plentiful. Our dogs were classified as yard dogs and hunting dogs. We had many different breeds at different times. The hunting dogs were usually some type of hounds and mixed breeds. There were German shepherds or collies for yard dogs. The dogs usually ate food from the table, wild game, or some dry store-bought food. The type of dog depended upon who claimed ownership. Men liked hounds; children liked pets.

Sometimes we had a goat but not always. Most likely my parents bought a nanny goat when my brother Jeremiah had to drink goat's milk as a young child. During my early childhood, we had a billy goat. The one thing that I remember about goats is that they will eat most anything. That includes paper, rags, wild plants, and the bark from the trees and clothes from the clothesline if they are not watched. Our billy goat was never too friendly to us children and would butt anyone if he got a chance.

Our cow furnished milk for the household. She had to be treated kindly and fed twice a day. Her production of milk and butter helped to feed a large family, plus dogs and cats. The cow ate grains, hay, and grass from the premises.

The many hogs and pigs lived within five hundred feet of our house. They kept meat and lard in our kitchen. They ate slop from the kitchen, lots of corn and oats. Sometimes they ate dry peas and hay. We were not allowed to become attached to a pig because they were our food. Cats roamed freely around the house. The cats ate any mice that came near our house or the barns. There was an entrance under the kitchen floor for the cat to come inside at will. The cats ate food from our table and drank a lot of milk.

Chickens helped to feed us; therefore, they got excellent care. Our chickens had freedom in the yard and surrounding gardening areas. There are a lot more facts about chickens in the *Food from the Barnyard* chapter.

There were times when my brothers would catch a little rabbit or squirrel and keep him. These animals were put in a cage and fed as if they belonged in the family.

Corn barn in 2011
Front View

Feed Shed in 2011
Early use Cow

Chapter 9

Downtown Swansea

Going Downtown

A former German village, Swansea was definitely a "farmers' town" during the 1940s and 1950s, located twenty-one miles from Lexington, Saint Matthews, and Columbia. Its name was derived from the German word for "twenty," and the very first house was constructed by Germans in 1886.

In 1890, Swansea experienced its first tragedy when, just south of the town limits, a southbound train's engineer failed to exit the railway and wait in town as directed. Many lives were lost when the northbound train slammed into it.

The railroad was very important to the community, with the Seaboard Air Line running through on the west side. Swansea was situated on the main railway line running from large northern cities such as New York, Boston, and Washington, to Miami, Florida. Water was supplied from a nearby pond to steam the locomotive's tanks. The town's railroad station also served as the Western Union office, and Mr. T. O. Setzler was the Depot Agent. Many freight trains stopped in Swansea because of the cotton and other businesses, while also carrying mail. Several passenger trains stopped daily.

My only train ride took place on our senior (high school) trip to Washington, D.C. Mama spoke about riding the train to Gaston when she was young—an eight-mile jaunt.

The main business district (Monmouth Avenue) was one block long, intersecting S.C. Hwy. #6 (Second Street) to the north and Third Street to the south. However, Monmouth Avenue stores were diverse.

In my mind's eye, travel with me from U.S. Hwy #321 (Church Street) southbound. Turn right on S.C. Hwy. #6 (Second Street), go two blocks, turn left on Monmouth Avenue. Simmons Grocery Store was the first store on the left corner. Upstairs was Dr. J. B. Edwards' office. The second store was Riley & Haigler, later renamed Haigler Brothers, which sold dry goods and groceries. The third store was Rast & Varn Dry Goods Store, with clothes, notions, shoes, and hosiery. Williams Hardware Store was next. I will tell you more about the hardware store a bit later.

Rubin & Schechter Dry Goods Store came next and would be considered a department store today. Clothes, kitchen items, and many other things, including some toys, could be found there. The sixth store was Sharpe Grocery. Mr. Sharpe was known for his fresh meat, because he butchered every week.

Next was W. L. Johnston Drug Store, where most prescriptions were filled for miles around. My mother told me that she had gone to school with Mrs. Julia Johnston. The store was fairly well equipped for its time, having a soda fountain and wrought-iron chairs around little round tables. Young people ked to come there.

The last store on the left of Monmouth Avenue was Bernstein Dry Goods Store, while Hill's Gulf Service Station sat on the corner. In the 1950s, this station also had a hot dog stand and young people could buy lunch for less than a quarter. In an earlier time, this lot was occupied by a Chevrolet place.

The (B. E.) Williams Hardware Store was managed by Mr. O'Neal Lybrand. It moved to Third Street later and operated as Lybrand Supply Company. The owner possessed several adjoining buildings for assembly of bicycles and other items. In my youth, Mr. Monroe Pinckney, a black man for whom the minority high school was later named, worked there. Mr. Pinckney knew all there was to know about the hardware business and had the respect of everyone, with no ethnic biases. Whenever someone needed a part for his farm equipment, Mr. Pinckney knew how to get it. The store not only sold regular hardware, but appliances, furniture, farming equipment, sporting goods, and toys. Mr. Pinckney must have been strong because he could handle heavy objects without straining himself. He was a quick thinker. I also remember the hardware store sold toys at Christmas time. Children like me enjoyed looking in the windows!

Imagine with me now to the other side of the street. Boozer Grocery was the first store on the right. My mother bought necessities there, trading excess eggs from the farm for other groceries. In the 1940s, the U.S. government issued food coupons (ration stamps) to families, with the number based upon how many people were in the family. Ration stamps were necessary to buy sugar, shortening, canned goods, and meats. There was a shortage of these things during the war, that I cannot remember well.

In the 1950s Mr. Boozer hired high school boys to deliver groceries after school in an old truck. Miss Sally Wise trained the Boozer boys to use the cash register. Some of the delivery boys I knew were Rhett Inabinet, C. L. Wise, and James Jumper. There was a rumor that, instead of giving these teenagers lunch or dinner breaks, Mr. Boozer fed them hamburgers cooked on an oil-burning stove.

The second store on the right was Craft Dime Store, where I remember buying bubble gum and hard candies for a penny each. Swansea Drug Store was next, flanked by a pool hall, since men did not own pool tables in those days. My family called them "beer joints," and ladies didn't go there frequently. As children, they were off limits.

The U.S. Post Office was next door, where Mr. Jackson Flake was the postmaster in the 1940s and 1950s. While Mr. Flake served in World War II, his wife was our postmistress. Their daughter, Sandra, was in my class and I knew the three other children also. Robert's Grocery was the last store on the right.

Facing Third Street and behind Robert's Grocery was Quitman Harley's Grocery. Thad Riley's business was behind Robert's Grocery and faced Cardiff Avenue at Third Street.

Most of these stores were heated with potbellied stoves and cooled by ceiling fans, far different from our country homes that still didn't have electric fans during the 1940s. In the 1940s and early 1950s, the main street was crowded with people of all ages on Friday evenings and all day on Saturdays. Monmouth Avenue became a place to shop and to visit other people who came to town at least once a week. The scene was marked by a community spirit—laughing and talking, catching up with the news and/or gossip. One unique custom came on Wednesday afternoons, when each store closed to allow employees time to go to church.

Another important business, Cleo William's Garage faced S.C. #6 (Second Street). He kept my dad's old A-model Ford, Hudson, and Chevrolet running for years. My brothers Floyd and H. P. learned a lot about cars from him. There was a liquor store behind William's Garage which faced Cardiff Avenue.

The Bank of Swansea faced Third Street, where the Town Hall now stands. Mrs. Melba Hoover's parents, Boynton E. Craft and Sallie Rast

Craft, were associated with the bank for years. The Swansea Theater, run by Mr. Lucius Martin and his sister Guyula Martin, faced Third Street. Mr. Martin was the projectionist and his sister sold tickets and popcorn and drinks. You could buy a movie ticket in early 1950s for nine cents and candy for a penny. Later in the 1950s Rhett Inabinet worked as projectionist at night.

Craig's Shoe Shop faced Third Street, as did The Barber Shop and Jowers Drinks.

Mr. Craig was quite congenial and knew his business well. I wore out a lot of heels walking from my parents' house to downtown Swansea to catch a Greyhound back to Columbia, and he would fix my shoes for nearly nothing. In 1955, after moving to Columbia in my early teens, I befriended his sister-in-law, Clarice Craig, and her daughter, Elizabeth. That's another story for a different time

The telephone company also faced Beacon Avenue. In an earlier time period, the telephone company was owned and operated by Dainty Cartin. However, if my memory serves me, Mr. A. O. Bolen owned and maintained the telephone company in the 1940s and 1950s. Incidentally, the phones were a far cry from what we use today. There were few desk type telephones and operators were summoned when there was an emergency. The telephone numbers were number one through four digits.

In the 1950s, H. L. Berry operated a Red & White grocery store facing S.C. #6. The town had really moved up a notch when that happened!

A very important part of the local economy was W. B. Rast Son's Company, where various-sized baskets were made and used by farmers all over. The thing I remember most about the factory was the whistle that blew at noon to signal lunchtime. This whistle was also used whenever any emergency occurred, such as a fire.

On the platform at the railroad station, cotton buyers tested cotton grade and made bids to the owners. There were several buyers, including the Riley Brothers and Mr. Bill Courtney. At least two cotton gins were on the outskirts of town. Corn was ground into meal and grits at the Swansea Milling Company, located on Hwy. #6. My dad went there frequently, and brother Horace worked there in the late 1940s.

The Methodist Church and Swansea First Baptist Church faced U.S. #321. Swansea First Baptist Church started as a "brush arbor" by H. B. Williams, Aline Courtney, and L. D. Corbitt. The Lutheran Church faced Lady Street.

There were various service stations and the Hilltop Restaurant along U.S. #321. A short distance farther south, on Hwy. #321 outside of town, was the log Community House. As noted earlier in this book, it was constructed by the WPA and served as the town's social hub. Directly across the highway was Ryan Ott Eatery.

The Witt Brothers lived downtown, owning hundreds of acres of farmland outside the town. Their home was situated on Church Street, where Lexington State Bank is now located. The brothers used heavy farm equipment and tools, long before most farmers had access to tractors or modern equipment.

These families comprised the social core of Swansea: Rast, Lybrand, Johnson, King, W. B. Williams, and Witt. Most social life revolved around families, churches, and school functions. With no televisions or air conditioning and few telephones, families seemed much closer-knit in those days. Although Swansea was small, it had its own policeman—Mr. Hass Spires in the 1940s and Mr. Senn in the 1950s.

Growing up with just life's bare necessities, I am reminded about the trust factor of that time. Since my family had good credit, we were allowed to buy on an account whatever my parents needed or wanted and did not have ready cash. When the money came in, they paid the creditors. I am really proud that my family's name was a name to be trusted in that way.

Regardless of color or creed, neighbors helped neighbors by sharing whatever they happened to have. While some folks referred to Swansea as "a one-horse town," it was pleasant and community centered. Some wonderful memories were made there.

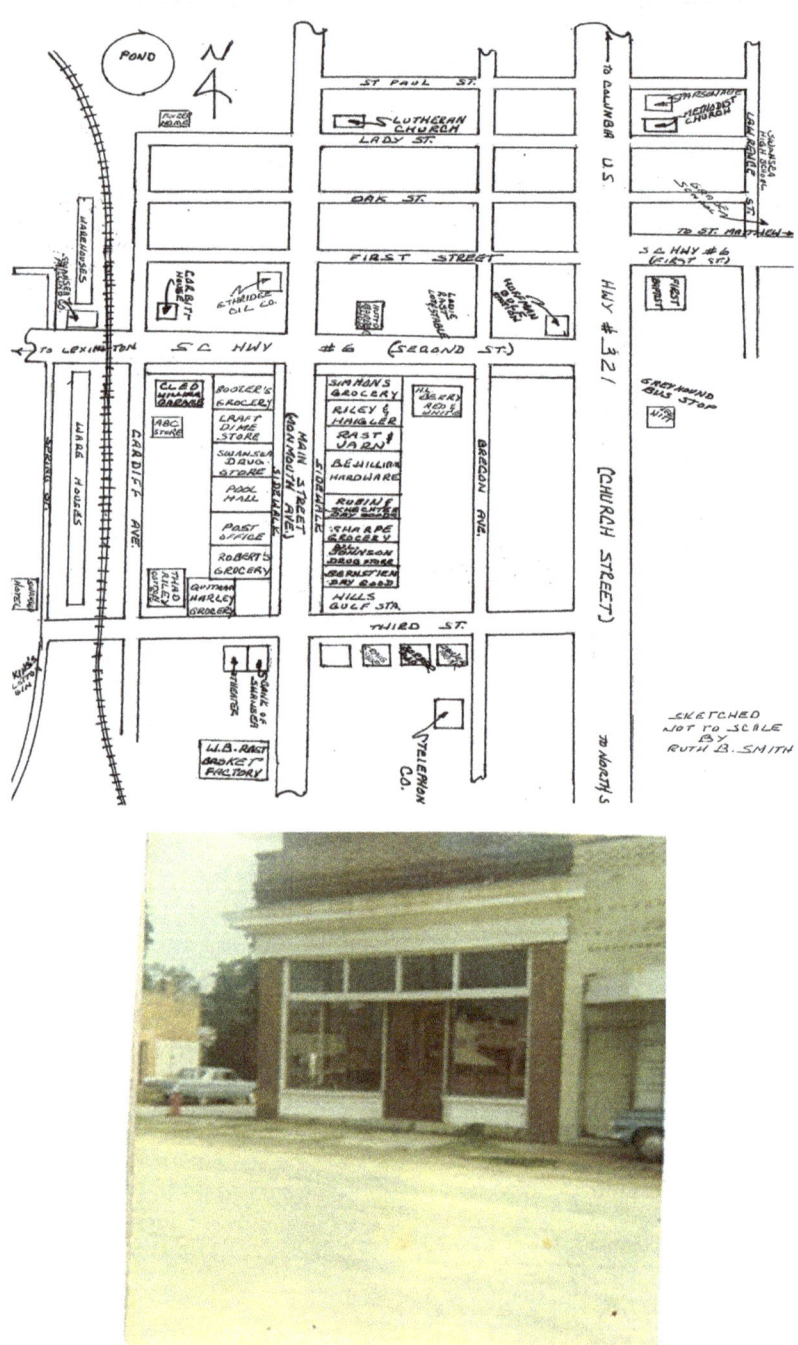

The Bank of Swansea in the forties
Used by permission Melba Hoover.

Continental Cotton Gin
Photo by James Busbee

Swansea Milling Company
Photo by James Busbee

PART 4
ACTIVITIES OF DAILY LIVING LARGE

Chapter 10

CLOTHING A *BIG* FAMILY

Clothes for Males

BOYS WORE OVERALLS (work clothes), but they were not as fashionable then as now. The denim material was tough and long lasting. Not only did they wear them to the fields, but also to school. Most of the time my brothers wore flannel shirts in the winter months. The flannel material was thick and much warmer than other available materials. When the men did not wear flannel, they wore chambray shirts. Chambray is a fine, lightweight type of gingham woven with white threads across a colored wrap. Most of the chambray shirts were a blue-gray color. Because of the direct heat from the sun, they usually wore long sleeves while working in the fields or gardens.

Most of the boys at our schools wore blue jeans, which were made of denim. Some of the boys from town wore khaki pants and a few of them wore dressier shirts.

Shoes were usually high-tops for work and/or school. My parents bought heavy shoes, which were expected to last a year. My dad repaired soles and heels on a tool resembling an anvil. His ability to mend shoes saved the family money. The only time the boys and Dad wore slippers was on Sundays or other very special occasions.

Most of the boy's and men's clothes and shoes were bought from local stores—Rubin and Schechter or Bernstein Dry Goods. Some things were bought from Sears and Roebuck catalogs. Back in the 1940s and 1950s catalog dealers would ship goods C.O.D. Ordering gave the buyer a little bit of lead time, just in case the money was not available immediately.

Sometimes the older boys outgrew their clothes. The outgrown overalls or shirts were handed down to a smaller boy. Our receivers always appreciated extra wearable clothes. Another thing that occurred often was patched pant legs. My mother patched the worn knees of pants and elbows of shirts. I find it fascinating, today, when my grandson deliberately buys jeans with holes in them from a high-priced store. This is now called stylish or classy. My brother and Mom called it necessity.

Socks were darned whenever holes appeared. Dad was good at darning holes. It is amazing how a hole can be filled with threads. No one seemed to mind wearing darned socks.

My dad always wore a dress shirt with a tie and dress pants on Sundays or special events. It was not unusual for the younger boys to wear jeans with a better shirt to church. You wore whatever you had. We were taught to wear our best to church. It was a way to respect God's house.

Girl and Ladies Clothes

Clothing the girls lent itself to more options. The very first option was hand-me-downs. The oldest girl probably got more new things, because she could not wear Mom's clothes. Whenever Dorcas outgrew clothes, she gave them to Esther. What Esther could not wear became mine. This practice had its advantages and disadvantages. Their clothes were newer, but I had more than they did. Some of our friends from school sometimes gave us used things. I remember one young lady (Janice Jeffcoat), who wore nice dresses and pretty skirts and sweaters, frequently gave Dot her slightly worn clothes. This act of kindness was so appreciated.

Many of the girls' dresses, jumpers, shirts, and skirts were homemade. They were either sewn on an old treadle sewing machine or hand-sewn. I remember my mother cutting her pattern for simple girl dresses. It seemed as if her favorite type of dress design opened down the front with buttons to the waistline and a gathered skirt. Peter Pan collars were most common back then. Many of these dresses were hand-sewn. She also liked jumpers and blouses. A jumper is a sleeveless garment with a square or low round neck. We always wore a shirt with them.

The sacks from chicken feed or some flour sacks in the 1940s and 1950s were very colorful. This material was always reused in some form or fashion. They came in a big assortment of colors and styles. You used whatever was available at little expense. There were a couple dry goods stores in Swansea that sold cloth by the yard. It was fun going shopping for material. The choices were much nicer than sacks.

One of my favorite memories of buying clothes was when we got to choose an outfit from the Sears Roebuck or Montgomery Ward catalog. We thought that was just so wonderful. These occasions were not too often. These buying sprees usually happened before Easter or Christmas when we had a little extra cash on hand. We were always thrilled when we were able to buy new sweaters. I liked pull-over sweaters with a small scarf.

The girls' and Mom's shoes were bought locally from one of the several dry goods stores on Main Street. Our shoes were bought large enough because they were expected to last about a year. For many years Lois and I could trade shoes but she outgrew me long before I left home. It was great while it lasted. I remember so well when Lois and I had the same

Mary Jane shoes but different colors. It was wonderful to change shoes at will. Maybe that is why I like shoes so much as an adult.

Wash Day

As far as washing clothes goes, we live in a magical time today. Wash day was a hard day's work. There was no magic about two very large tin tubs and scrub boards. We had no heated water unless it was heated on the wood kitchen stove or the iron washpot. In my early days, everything was washed by hand. My mother bought large boxes of washing powder from the general store and used homemade lye soap or Octagon Soap. The lye soap was made from the tallow extracted from the butchered hogs and lye. The scrub boards were indispensable.

Wash day began early in the morning because it was an all-day ritual. Whenever there were a lot of white clothes, the old iron washpot was filled with water and heated. The clothes were separated into two big piles and taken to the wash area outside. During the winter the large tubs were placed on a long bench outside near the chimney.

This was the warmest side of the house because it faced south. The tubs were filled with water, one for washing and the other for rinsing. On the really cold days, kettles of boiling water were put in them to take the chill from the freshly pumped water.

Each and every piece of clothing was put into the sudsy tub of water and scrubbed. If any soiled spots were noticed, lye soap was applied and rescrubbed hard on the scrub board. Whoever was in charge paid close attention to the collars and cuffs, which seemed to become the dirtiest. The item was then placed in the rinse tub. White clothing was boiled in the old iron washpot (the same pot was used for butchering and making soap). Boiling the clothes did away with any dinginess or lackluster appearance. With so few extras, we needed to keep them bright as long as possible. Whenever the wash water became too dirty or discolored, it had to be poured on the ground, usually in a flower bed and replaced. (I still own Mom's old washpot that we made into a table with a glass top.)

Sometime the men's overalls or coveralls that were extremely soiled were put on a bench and beaten with a paddle to loosen the grime or dirt. This did not happen all the time but was not uncommon. The thick denim used in blue jeans, overalls, and coveralls was very heavy and difficult to wash by hands alone.

Rinsing was a "piece of cake." Wringing out the clothes was more difficult, especially the men's heavy clothing. Hanging up the clothes was a lot more fun. We had several lines made of heavy wire between two poles. The clothespins were made of wood with a slit in the middle. Their tops looked like a little ball. Each item was hung in its own special way. Shirts were pinned on the line by the tail of the shirt, pants by the hem or cuff, dresses by the shoulders. The white clothes that had been boiled were rinsed and then hung as any others. Freshly washed and sun-dried clothes always smelled good.

It may come as a shock to most modern-day wives, but each week I still hang my bed linens to sun dry. The country in me just won't die easily.

Care was taken folding the clothes as they were removed from the line. Most of the clothes, if folded correctly, needed little or no ironing. Better clothes were put on hangers immediately, because no one liked unnecessary ironing.

My very first credit purchase after going to work for Southern Bell Telephone Company was a roller-type washing machine for my mother. It was a defining moment for me as a young teenager and a grand event for Mom. The year was 1955.

My parents had been married almost forty years and washed thousands of loads of clothes. In retrospect, I am thankful my priorities were right. Mom deserved the very best gift.

Ironing the Clothes

Before farms had electricity, the clothes were pressed with old-fashioned flat irons. Only the essential clothes were ironed because the appliance (flat iron) was not a lot of fun. The irons were heated on the wood stove in the kitchen or in front of the open fireplace. My memory is not really sharp on the ironing process.

Only the Sunday clothes were ironed. White shirts were starched in Argo starch, hung on the line to dry, and sprinkled to make them damp again, after which, they were pressed with the flat iron. It is quite difficult to get the temperature right. The wood stove got the irons either too hot or not hot enough. A happy medium was hard to obtain. No wonder some people called those sadirons. The "sad" means heavy; however, the other meaning of the word could apply to many young brides who never thought it could apply to her task. I remember my mom and oldest sister placing a piece of clothing on the edge of a bed and running the hot iron across the surface of the shirt or skirt.

Many of these irons have been relegated to the shelf as collector's items. As soon as electricity became available, those old flat irons were the first to go. Now, the best use for a sadiron is as a door stop. Then you must hope some child's curiosity doesn't get the best of her and it falls on a toe. Many of my friends find it amazing that I still iron starched shirts.

Chapter 11

Seating a Houseful

The Table

Many people would find it impossible or laughable to feed eleven people three meals a day at the same table. My oldest brother got married a year before the youngest was born. For a short span, eleven people, including two parents, ate at our table.

The kitchen table was about eight feet long and three- to four-feet wide and probably homemade. It had four square legs approximately thirty inches in height. A leg was near each of the four corners of the tabletop.

Our table was built sturdy. The lumber used in construction was about an inch thick, well sanded, and had a brown finish. Mom kept an oil cloth on the table at all times. Many of the cloths were plaid or checkered but varied. Whenever the tablecloth was frayed or worn, a new one, sold by the yard, was purchased from the hardware or general store.

The seating arrangement was most interesting. A long backless bench about eight feet long was placed on each side. One bench was against the wall. Those fortunate enough to get a back row seat could lean back on the wall and relax. The benches were built sturdy from ordinary lumber that matched the table. A lone chair was placed at each end of the table. Dad sat at the head of the table (north end) and Mom sat at the other end (south end). The siblings were arranged as the parents saw fit. There were few changes in the seating arrangement, and with good reason. Some naturally got along better with certain others. Any bickering between siblings created a move or quick discipline. I happened to be one of the lucky ones and got to sit against the wall. Even today I can recall quite well finishing my meal before most of the others. With permission, I literally crawled under the table between feet to get free.

In our household, everyone was required to eat together unless there was a legitimate reason for not being present. Breakfast was ready between 6:30 and 7:00 a.m. Lunch was served between 12 noon and 1 p.m. The evening meal varied more than the other meals because it depended on those working in the fields. The workers worked as late as possible during the busy seasons. The younger school children, who did not eat lunch at school, ate whenever they got home around 2:30 p.m. The most important thing that I remember about every meal was the blessing of the food (prayer). Usually, my dad asked the blessing, but occasionally, someone else would. There were no exceptions to the cardinal rule of prayer at all meals. Even if it was peanut butter and saltines with buttermilk on Saturday nights, someone asked God's blessing.

Mealtime was a time to get caught up on the happenings of the day. We needed to be aware about what the rest of the family was doing. That time was a good time to reflect on what really mattered in life. We really needed the favor of the Lord as survival. When someone started eating too quickly, we were reminded that our hogs gobbled up whatever was put before them, without so much as lifting a head to acknowledge from where it came. It may not be a good comparison, but that was the way it was taught to us children.

Storage

Storage in the kitchen for a large family was scarce. Near the south end of our long eating table sat the old but valuable pie safe. There were no cabinets as we know today. This piece of furniture was made of wood painted in a medium brown tone. The front of the safe was made of metal, probably tin. In this metal front were many small holes that looked somewhat like ice pick holes. The holes were to let air flow through the piece of furniture to keep the food stored there as fresh as possible under the existing conditions. The temperature was rather warm in our family home.

Not only was food stored in our pie safe, but dishes and flatware were also kept there. The china we used was quite simple, mostly plain white stoneware. Stoneware, such as we used, was heavy and lasted for a very long time. Some of the dishes may have had some designs, but not a lot of color. The flatware that I remember was also simple. The handles were made of wood with brads in them to hold the tins or spoons in place. Some of the glassware was purchased with Octagon soap coupons. These coupons could be saved and traded for usable objects for the household.

The drinking glasses, along with the plates, cups, saucers, and bowls, were stored on a shelf in the top section of the pie safe. Flatware was stored in a drawer that was the width of the safe. Underneath the metal-covered portion of the safe were several large round tin containers where flour, rice, cornmeal, and lard were stored. Due to the size of our family, all commodities were bought in very large quantities. It was not unusual to buy flour or rice in fifty-pound bags. Sugar was bought in ten-pound bags when it was not rationed. During World War II, you bought whatever was allocated.

A few years ago my daughter and I went out for lunch. She suggested we eat at a place in Columbia Mall that she was excited about. When we got there, it reminded me of home sixty-plus years ago. The tables were covered with checkered oil cloth and the drinking glasses were pint jars. She thought it was so "cool" and I thought "I've been there and done that." The food was good but surely was a backward glance to my young days.

Aprons

Anyone cooking in Mom's kitchen was expected to wear an apron. Mom always wore a bibbed apron when in the kitchen. Her aprons were usually made from feed sacks. Which were very colorful with many different designs. Some of her aprons were made of heavier materials. Evidently, she made aprons from whatever material was available at little or no cost to her.

Aprons protected the dresses from stains or spills in the kitchen. They kept soot produced by the stove from messing up dresses that were worn over and over again. Whenever someone came to visit, she removed her apron and welcomed her guest.

The women were so used to wearing aprons that even in the 1960s, Lois and I made aprons and sold them to raise funds for missions around the world. Ours were much more modern and stylish than our mother's aprons.

PART 5
THE THINGS WE TAKE FOR GRANTED

Chapter 12

Utilities or Lack Thereof

The Outhouse

Some call it a privy (a toilet). Others may say it's a backhouse. But I call it an outhouse. An outhouse is a building separate from but located near a main building or dwelling; a small structure used for defecating or urinating, typically having a seat or seats with a hole over a deep pit.

The outhouse on our farm was behind our barn. It was a couple hundred feet from the back door of the farmhouse. The structure was made of unfinished lumber and had a tin roof. Its approximate measurements were six feet wide, four or five feet in depth, and about six or seven feet in height. The flooring was rough lumber. The largest boards in it were the corner posts that were made from two-by-fours. Its roof was taller on the front side and slanted downward to the back.

On the inside was a raised structure about two feet from the floor. It protruded about two feet from the back outside wall. In this raised structure were three round cutout holes. Underneath the building was a deep hole. The hole held the human waste from the household. One cheerful aspect of the outdoor toilet was its door; it had a half-moon cut out on the door. Last year's Sears and Roebuck catalog hung from a nail on the wall. Some outhouses had only two seats instead on three.

On a cold moonless night, going to the outhouse was a bit scary. For the less venturesome person, we always had at least one chamber pot in the house. The chamber pot was a galvanized pot with a removable lid. This pot fit under a bed and was used in emergencies. Some of the more elite families owned a potty chair similar to the ones used in our hospitals or rest homes when the patient is unable to reach a traditional bathroom. Some chamber pots were quite elegant with beautiful designs. Even those in high offices had their own chamber pot, such as Winston Churchill and President Roosevelt.

Most all the homes in our area had outhouses in the 1940s and 1950s. Some of the homes in the Swansea town limits had these outside structures into the decades covered in this book. Many of the homes owned by the more affluent families, who had electricity and running water, still had the country feel to them well into the twentieth century.

There still are many humorous stories about the outhouse where we lived. I want to share a few. The rumors were that my brothers smoked corn silk cigarettes or rabbit tobacco out back. The matches used to light the homemade cigarette were thrown in the hole and caught the paper below on fire. That was scary! My worst very real experience was when a wasp stung me on my rump. Not only was it painful and embarrassing, I got quite nervous because my sister Lois had serious allergic reactions to bee stings.

This poem is a good description of what our outhouses were like. (Used by permission)

My Favorite Old-Time Poem

The Passing of the Old Backhouse

When memory keeps me company
and moves to smiles or tears,
A weather-beaten object looms
throughout the mist of years,
Behind the house and barn it stood,
a half a mile or more—
And hurrying feet a path had made
straight for its swinging door.

Its architecture was a type
of simple classic art,
But in the tragedy of life
it played a leading part,
And oft' the passing traveler
drove slow and heaved a sigh,
to see the modest hired girl
slip out with glances shy.

We had our posy garden
that the women loved so well.
I loved it, too, but better still,
I loved the stronger smell,
that filled the evening breezes
so full of homely cheer,
And told the night-o'ertaken tramp
that human life was near.

On lazy August afternoons,
it made a little bower,
Delightful, where my grandsire sat
and whiled away an hour,
For there the summer mornings
its very cares entwined,
And berry bushes reddened
in the steaming soil behind.

All day fat spiders spun their webs
to catch the buzzing flies
That flitted to and from the house
where Ma was baking pies,
And once a swarm of hornets bold
had built a palace there,
And stung my unsuspecting aunt
—I must not tell you where.

Then father took a flaming pole
—that was a happy day,
He nearly burned the building down,
but the hornets left to stay.
When summer bloom began to fade
and winter to carouse,
We banked the little building
with a heap of hemlock boughs.

And when the crust was on the snow
and the sullen skies were gray,
In sooth the building was no place
where one could wish to stay,
We did our duties promptly,
there one purpose swayed our mind,
We tarried not, nor lingered long
on what we left behind.

The torture of that icy seat
would make a Spartan sob,
For needs must scrape the gooseflesh
with a lacerating cob,
That from a frost-encrusted nail
was suspended by a string—
My father was a frugal man
and wasted not a thing.

When Grandpa had to "go out back"
and make his morning call,
We'd bundle up the dear old man
with a muffler and a shawl,
I knew the hole on which he sat—
'twas padded all around,
And once I dared to sit there—
'twas all too wide I found.

My loins were all too little,
and I jack-knifed there to stay.
They had to come and pry me out
or I'd have passed away.
Then Father said ambition was
a thing that boys should shun,
And I must use the children's hole
till childhood days are done.

And still I marvel at the craft
that cut those holes so true;
The baby hole, and the slender hole
that fitted Sister Sue,
The dear old country landmark;
I've tramped around a bit,
And in the lap of luxury
my lot has been to sit.

But ere I die I'll eat the fruit
of trees I robbed of yore,
Then see the shanty where my name
is carved upon the door,
I ween the old familiar smell
will soothe my faded soul,
I'm now a man, but nonetheless,
I'll try the children's hole.

—Generally attributed to
James Whitcomb Riley

Light / Sources of Light

We frequently take light for granted because it is so common. No matter how common light may seem, we cannot live without it. The light from the sun heats the earth. God created such a wonderful cycle when he spoke light upon his creation. From the very beginning of time as the earth knew it, man tried to find ways of making light when there was no sunlight.

Light from whatever source makes it possible for us to see. Examples of sources of light are the sun and a lighted candle. We see because light from a source travels to our eyes. Light is either natural or artificial. We usually think of the sun and stars as the only natural light, but some living things, such as fireflies and some bacteria also produce natural light. Our artificial light comes from sources that man controls.

From my earliest memory, we had artificial light at night and the early morning. Our sources in my earliest days were primitive. We used kerosene lamps and Coleman lanterns. The lamps were made of glass with a medal midsection that held the wick. The base of the lamp was composed of two sections. Its bottom was round and flat so it could sit on a table or other furniture. Then it came upward forming a reservoir to hold the kerosene. The midsection was formed somewhat like an hourglass; this section held the metal section where the wick was positioned. On top of the metal wick holder was a glass shade. The shade was usually clear glass but sometimes had a design on it.

The wick in a lamp will get frayed after burning for a while. At least once a week someone in the family must trim the lamp and refill it with kerosene. The person refilling a lamp must be very careful not to overrun the lamp bowl. If the wick were not trimmed straight, or if it had some debris on it, the lamp shade would quickly smoke up. We never wanted that to happen, because it made for a real inconvenience for the whole family. Of course, we had other lamps in the house most of the time. A dirty shade was not any fun.

We children played games with the shadows from the light. With hands together and thumbs held high, the shadow on the wall looked somewhat like a horse. We also made rabbit shapes and church steeples. The older kids had a knack for shadow playing. The shadows in the glow of a flickering lamp can be relaxing. During my early childhood, I saw some wonderful things in the glow of our lamps.

The men in the Busbee family went hunting at night. They always took a hunting lantern with them. There were several different types. We owned a Coleman lantern that was also used inside the home. Its light was much brighter, because it had a different kind of wick. The light was white light instead of a more yellow light from the regular lamps and lanterns. Lanterns have wicks that must be kept trimmed just like the lamps. I cannot remember the Coleman lantern wick having to be changed. These lanterns also burned kerosene.

Life became easier in 1949 when South Carolina Electric and Gas Company finally installed an electric line on JonesWire Road. We had better lighting, even if it was just a bulb hanging from the ceiling. Each room had one light to begin with and we thought we had gone to heaven! What a big difference we experienced. A sixty-watt bulb gave off much more light than any of our lamps. No more lamp washing or wick trimming. We felt as though the sun shone indoors or some other miracle. We were quite excited to have new light. My parents were cost- conscious and would remind us to turn off the light. However, I liked to stay up later studying, after the others went to bed.

Saturday Bath

Every Saturday Mom or Dot would heat water on the woodstove for our baths. A big galvanized tub was placed in front of the fireplace, filled with boiling water and enough cold water to get the right temperature for the girls to take a bath. We all used the same tubful of water to get our baths. The four girls took turns getting all washed up. If our hair was dirty, it was washed while in the tub. Whenever we washed our hair, we had to let it air-dry. Soap was used to wash the hair as well as the body. Sometimes vinegar was rinsed through the wet hair to make it shiny and easier to comb.

Another practical object in our home was the wash basin. This object sat on a wash table in the kitchen near the back door. Several buckets of water with a dipper sat on this table. Towels were hung within reach of the table. A rule at our home was that "everyone washed their hands when coming in for meal time." Some basins were fancy. These basins were also used for sponge baths throughout the week. The buckets used for bringing in the water varied from plain to fancy. Ours were simple.

Clean Water

Many people think that water is free. That seems logical; however, one must pay to get clean water or work for it as we did in my parents' home. Water is the most common substance on the face of the earth. We have oceans, rivers, lakes, and groundwater. Life could not exist without water. No plants, animals, fish, fowl, or mankind would survive without this precious substance. The people on earth are either slave or master of water. We need water in our homes, factories, and irrigation systems.

The fresh water in the Busbee home came from a pitcher pump. This pump was called a lift pump and was the simplest reciprocating pump.

Sometimes this simple system is called a suction pump because it creates a partial vacuum that lifts the water from the well or underground stream. There was a piston in the cylinder. The piston had a valve that opens as the piston moves down and closes when it moves up. At the bottom of the water pipe that extends into the well or water stream, there is another valve called a pressure valve. The bottom valve closes and prevents the water from flowing downward.

The valves will not work unless they are airtight. The person getting water pumps the handle (moves it up and down) until the bucket or barrel is filled. Sometimes, in the winter, the top valve in the pump would freeze. In order to get water, hot water would have to be poured into the top cylinder of the pump to thaw the ice. After a few minutes the shrunk valve would expand and create the vacuum to make the water flow. The clean, fresh water came slowly at first then much faster as it ran freely into the open buckets. The type of equipment that we used is termed a shallow well system. Because we lived near a major creek, the water was no more than thirty-five or forty feet deep. This water was always cold and refreshing. Just inside the kitchen door was a table where buckets of water were always kept. The whole family drank water from the dipper that stayed in or near the water pail. We used galvanized or enamel dippers. Some of our neighbors made dippers from gourds. They looked strange but served their purpose.

From this same pump, all of the farm animals were watered. In the hot weather, this chore seemed to never end. Carrying buckets of water to the horses, cow, hogs, chickens, and dogs was a back-breaking chore. We all helped with this major task. It finally occurred to me why none of the Busbee children were overweight. We got plenty of exercise pumping water.

Chapter 13

KEEPING WARM OR COOL

Our Fireplace

TIME SPENT IN front of a crackling fireplace warms me on the inside. Just watching the fire lifts my spirit. Much work must be done before the enjoyment of sitting in front of the fire can happen. Trees or limbs must be cut from the woods or our swamp areas and hauled to our wood pile that was kept several hundred feet from the home. Wood had to be cut and stacked. Someone had to be held responsible each day to bring in enough to last through the night. Our fireplace required wood twenty-four to thirty inches long. Isn't it amazing that cutting wood warms you and burning wood also warms you? In the bygone days, we either worked or froze. There were never any icicles on any of us. You cut wood or you were cold.

In some of the more modern fireplaces, open ducts are placed at the sides of the fireplace. The higher ducts give off warm air and help heat the room. Central heating has become more common in the United States than in most other countries. Local heating is still in common use in many countries.

The very earliest type of local heating system was the open fire within an enclosure, such as a cave or a tent. That system was not satisfactory, because the area became filled with smoke. The open fire, without a chimney, did not have enough draft to burn well. A fireplace with a chimney put at one side or corner of a room caused the smoke and combustion gases to pass up the chimney to increase the burning.

The fireplace in our old-time country home was the focal point in the living room. The opening with its grate was probably thirty-six to forty inches wide. There were bricks on the interior and the hearth. Inside the opening there was a damper, which allowed the smoke to go up the chimney and exit outside higher than the roof. The damper is an instrument used to adjust the flow of heat. When the damper was wide-open, the wood burned faster and produced an intense heat. The damper could be partially closed to keep the fire burning longer.

The outside of the chimney was made of large stones of various sizes held in place with mortar. The lowest level of the chimney was five or six feet wide. The width of the structure lessened as it went upward. At the top, it was probably about three feet in width and nearly the same in depth. This was the common size at that time.

By morning, the temperature in the house dropped considerably. We took turns, and the person who awakened first started the fire if it was completely out. There were small pieces of lightwood used especially for kindling. Matches were made readily available for the lucky person. Heat didn't remain very long in our house. Like most houses built years ago, it wasn't properly insulated. The few homes in our area were insulated with layers of newspaper inside the walls.

I must admit that I have some wonderful memories of sitting around that old rustic fireplace. One of our parents would put raw sweet potatoes under the red coals and ashes at the bottom of the grate and roast them while we enjoyed the evening together. Sometimes we heated water for baths in an old iron kettle on the hearth. Most often, Mom or my older sisters would heat the old-fashioned flatirons in front of the fire. One of my nephews, who is now deceased, told me years ago that roasting potatoes in the open fireplace was his fondest childhood memory. Many nights while sitting around, our dad would read to us or we would talk about things heard or that had happened.

Another kind of heating system that was quite common in the 1940s and 1950s was cast-iron or other heavy metal stoves that sat upright in the living room or dining area of the country home. This type of stove had a six- or eight-inch metal pipe going up through the ceiling or a side wall to a flue. Our great American statesman and inventor Benjamin Franklin developed the Franklin stove in the early 1740s. His creation was a cast-iron enclosure fitted into a fireplace. It extended into the room on three sides and gave off heat. My parents did not have one of these stoves, but my brother H. P. had one.

Most of these heating stoves were wood-burning; however, some of them were coal-burning. The iron stoves seemed to give a more intense heat and could warm the room quicker than a fireplace. My oldest brother H. P., who lived about a half mile from my parents, had a wood-burning stove during the 1940s until sometime in the sixties. His family burned wood in their stove. On the front of their stove were knobs that were adjusted for air intake similar to our fireplace damper. Ashes had to be removed frequently to prevent a buildup that could cause a house fire.

H. P. with his wood stove

Quilts and More Quilts

The quilt is a bedcover made of two layers of cloth filled with down, cotton, or wool. Our home had many different kinds of quilts. Each of our beds had three or four quilts in the coldest part of the winter. Some of the beds in our home were feather beds. These beds were exceptionally warm in the winter, because you felt as if the mattress made with feathers partially swallowed you. The sheets were made of flannel and it seemed as if they held the heat. At least they felt soft and cozy.

My aunt Gertrude, Mom's sister, had a special frame set up in her house where she quilted. The ones in our home were made of cotton or wool scraps pieced together with a design or pattern. The bottom layer was usually a solid color that blended with the top layer. Aunt Gertrude used batting as the center layer of the quilts she made.

The three layers were stretched out on a rectangular quilting frame to keep the fabrics smooth and in shape. The stitches followed a design marked on the top layer of cloth. Very small stitches were used to prevent the interlining from slipping. The entire cover was quilted before it could be taken from the frame. After the quilting was finished, the edges were bound with bias strips of cloth. Some fancy quilts could have been finished with pretty ribbon as binding tape.

Some of the quilts we used were quite old even at that point in time. Whenever we needed more covers, Mom would have Aunt Gertrude make more quilts. She was a blessing to our family, and she also made some spending money.

Back in the 1940s and 1950s, organized groups of ladies made quilts for charitable purposes. They were known as Quilting Bees. Not only were the quilts made at these meetings useful, but the bees were an awesome social outlet for the women. Some of these ladies' husbands were in the military during the war and were gone for long periods of time. There were also some young and old widows. Even today, there is an active Quilting Bee south of Swansea on Highway #3. Their quilts are still made for fun and are given away to needy causes.

There were special racks made just for quilts in many homes. The heirloom quilts were passed from one generation to another. Some of these quilts were super eloquently designed and became very valuable. Some of my family has quilt racks in their guest bedrooms. What we once considered a necessity can now be our treasured asset. On a few occasions when a child didn't feel well, Mom would wrap a heated brick in a towel and put it under the covers. This did not happen often and seemed a bit drastic. The brick would hold the heat for a long period of time.

Layers of clothes

This may sound absurd, but in the dead of winter on the coldest of days, we all wore long johns or union suits. Most everyone is familiar with insulated underwear for hunters or outdoorsmen. However, in the olden days, there was a girl's version. This was one piece of underwear that covered the legs to the ankles. It had snaps up the bodice front and had long sleeves. There was a flap in the back with snapper grippers used when going to the bathroom. Even though they were not pretty, I must admit they were warm. The boys' version sometimes came in two pieces.

The boys/men wore overalls or coveralls over their long johns. When the girls wore long johns, they wore long socks or hose that came over the knees. I always hated these long stockings and thought they made us children look like old women. The boys always wore high-top shoes. We girls always wore dresses or skirts and blouses or pullover sweaters. Most of the time the guys wore flannel shirts for work or school. Over these shirts, they wore thick sweaters or denim jackets. The girls wore the warmest outer garments that were available. The outer coats and jackets were handed down until they were worn out and threadbare.

Warm weather was always welcomed. The girls felt liberated with our penny loafers or saddle-oxfords and we could, at last, wear regular socks. Many mornings we got dressed in the kitchen where the cook stove warmed the place. This was not the best arrangement but we were warm.

Keeping cool

Umbrella-like chinaberry trees shaded an outdoor table where we used to eat and work. The chinaberry is a tropical Asiatic tree belonging to the mahogany family, bearing yellow, beadlike fruit. It is widely grown as a lawn tree throughout the southern United States. These trees are very large and offer a dense shade. When it was almost unbearably hot inside, it always seemed cooler with a breeze under these trees. The long table under these trees was on a permanent footing. It was constructed of rough lumber that had been smoothed with a plane. There was no paint or finishing product on it. It was fairly high off the ground. There were no seats around it. Since this table was primarily a work area, we stood up when we ate there. This is the same table we used to prepare food for canning.

One of my dad's all-time favorite treats was served on this table. He tried extra hard to have yellow watermelons ripe by the Fourth of July celebration. The family kept the seeds from one year until the next. The yellow watermelon seemed to be much sweeter than its red counterpart. We raised these watermelons and cantaloupes in our regular garden plots, rather than large acreage used for profit.

Many times, after lunch was cleared from the outdoor table, some of us children would climb onto the table and take an afternoon nap. The family rested several hours during the middle of the day. While the children napped outside, our parents napped on the bed with windows wide open, hoping for a breeze.

Paper fans, given to us by Thompson Funeral Home in West Columbia, were a real blessing. We not only used them while sitting around at home, but also used them at church. Few of the smaller churches in the area had electric fans, but no air conditioners. The fans also helped us deal with gnats during the hot August dog days of summer.

The hot summers would have been unbearable without the swimming hole at the creek. The cold water was the only place to really get cool. Air conditioners were something we dreamed about. Bull Swamp Creek was at the east boundary of the Busbee farm. We walked about a thousand feet through the horse pasture in back of the family home into the swampy area in order to get to the creek. The men had cut a good-sized path into the wooded area to the stream. The path was five or six feet wide and approximately one hundred feet long. This is the spot where we jumped into the icy water just to cool off. Whenever we really wanted to swim, we walked about a half mile to Nulty Crossing for the plunge. At this location, a county road crossed the creek. Our family dug out the stream to make a good-sized swimming hole. (See Fun and Play story.)

Some of my fondest memories revolve around Bull Swamp Creek. I cannot emphasize too strongly how important this creek was to our survival in the extreme heat. It was in the dugout swimming hole that I learned to swim. We took watermelons with us and put them in the running water while we swam and played. When we were tired of playing, the watermelons were burst open. The juicy red or yellow fruit was so refreshing. Occasionally, we would cook out on the banks of the stream. It was much cooler under the dense shade than at home.

There was another much smaller stream we called a branch or rill on our property.

It was around four or five hundred feet from the house, it had ankle deep water in which we could wade. Here, also, is where we washed the turnips for market in the fall. It was a fun place for young children.

Chapter 14

THE PRIZED APPLIANCES

The Kitchen Stove

THE MOST SOCIALIZED space in the Busbee home was in the kitchen, around Mom's old-time wood stove. This stove not only cooked our meals, it warmed our water and served as storage for leftover biscuits and baked potatoes. It was made of wrought iron with a bit of porcelain on it. The porcelain probably was for looks only.

Facing the stove on its left side was the hot water tank. The tank was attached strategically to the main frame of the stove near the chamber where the firewood burned. In that way, the water heated faster since it was adjoined to the heating chamber. Not all water tanks were on the left side, many were on the right side of the stove. The flat surface on top of the stove had four burners. These were round iron circles cut from the heavy iron surface. Each had a notched place where it could be removed from the stove with its metal lifter. The lifter had cut-outs on the smaller end that fit perfectly into the notched eye or burner. Whenever a pot or frying pan did not seem to be heating fast enough, the burner could be removed and the container placed in the direct path of the heat.

Beneath the heat chamber was another door with a damper in it. The damper could be opened to cause the fire to burn faster. Ashes were also removed from the stove by opening the bottom door. The use of the damper could regulate the heating process.

The oven was a large chamber with a metal shelf in the middle of the open space. Our oven was about two-thirds the width of the stove and was under the upper burners. The oven would hold a half-bushel of sweet potatoes at one time. Sometimes several dishes were prepared at one time. This cut down on the time spent over a hot stove We cooked biscuits or corn bread three times a day. We also made tasty cobblers and pies in this oven. One who has lived through my upbringing has a real appreciation for electricity.

Near the stove, which sat at an angle between two kitchen windows, was the wood box. Every day someone had to cut wood into about twelve- to fifteen-inch-long pieces. The lucky child whose turn it was to cut the wood had to cut enough to last for cooking three meals. Our wood box sat directly under the window on the right wall. The woodpile is where my dad and/or older brothers brought tree limbs, or small trees from the forest or swamp on our property, to a designated location about a hundred feet from the backyard.

The younger sibling, who was responsible on a given evening, would use an ax and chop a stack of twelve- to fifteen-inch pieces about two feet in width and about one foot in depth. We also had to bring in some lightwood for starting the fire. Lightwood is from dead pine trees. The kindling wood is very dense and will ignite quickly.

From my earliest memory, Mama made biscuits every day. She would knead dough until it was soft and elastic. Whenever she bought flour, it was bought in a fifty-pound sack. She used a certain deep wooden bowl for making homemade bread. Her biscuit pans were very heavy metal ones. Sometimes she used a porcelain one. She would pinch off a small piece of dough about the size of a large plum and roll it in her hands until it felt right to her, then she would put it on the greased pan. When the pan was filled to her satisfaction, she would press each piece of dough with the palm of her hand to flatten them. Her biscuits were wonderfully crispy, but still light.

The metal frame of the stove rose about two feet above the cooking surface. At the top of this framework were two compartments extending the entire width of the stove. These compartments extended toward the front of the stove about one foot to eighteen inches. These extensions were known as the warming closet. It was in these stove closets that Mom stowed away the leftover biscuits and always had warm snacks, such as baked potatoes, for her children's snacks. We sometimes got a biscuit, bored a hole in the top of it, and filled the hole with syrup or jelly. Some of my brothers liked to cut the bread in half and put a slice or slices of tomato in the middle.

All wood-burning kitchen stoves have a six- or eight-inch metal pipe attached to the flat cooking surface. This pipe, which carries soot and combustion gases outside, usually had an elbow near the ceiling that extended through the wall into a flue that was on top of the roof. Care was taken not to overheat the pipe in the wall and cause a serious fire. Most of the pots and pans were made of cast iron. Food tasted so good cooked in them. My family kept these utensils until that house burned in 1966.

Wood-burning stove, photo by James Busbee

Our Icebox

With no electricity, refrigeration was difficult at best. However, we used what we had, and that happened to be an upright icebox. Our icebox was about four feet tall. It was approximately three-feet wide and about two-and-a-half feet in depth. The upper part was the chamber that held a fifty-pound block of ice. During that time period men drove ice trucks into the areas of the cities or towns that did not have modern refrigerators. These drivers came into our neighborhood, frequently. Otherwise, ice could be bought at an icehouse in towns.

The top section on the icebox opened by lifting the lid that was hinged from the back edge of the box. In order to use the block of ice stored in this box, we used an ice pick. One must be very careful not to hurt anyone with this instrument. Whoever was preparing the meal would chip off the block in small chunks just enough for everyone eating. We were careful not to be wasteful. Our icebox was not as fancy as some, but I remember how practical it was then. It was painted blue on the outside. The bottom section had a door that opened outward from its front hinges. In this compartment, we stored milk and anything else that would spoil easily, such as butter, cheese, and meats. Most of the fruits and vegetables were prepared on a daily basis.

A copper tube ran from the upper ice block chamber through the perishable food chamber and out beneath the icebox. We kept a drip pan on the floor under the tubing to catch the water coming from the melting ice before it got on the floor. This pan had to be emptied almost every day. Should we forget to empty it, we had a puddle on the floor.

Whenever anyone complained about having to empty the pan, we were reminded that anything worth having was worth the work. This old adage stuck with me when I was tempted to give up on a hard task. It taught me gratitude and fortitude. Use what you have and work hard to make things better.

Just yesterday, while going to my volunteer job, I saw a man with no legs, but he was wearing two prosthetics. This guy was trying to run down Farrow Road, crossing over I-77. It was a humbling sight to see such courage. I am so grateful that I always had two good legs and always had the ability to get store-bought ice. What a blessing! While many people in our world do not have clean water to drink, I can drink ice-cold beverages.

Our Entertainment Center

During the early period of my life, radio broadcasting held much of the same role in family entertainment as television has today. From the 1920s through the 1940s and well into the 1950s, families throughout most of the United States gathered around their radios most nights. In fact, this period is often referred to as the *Golden Age of Broadcasting*. This era did not end until television came on the scene in the 1950s.

During my childhood, the radio had dramas, light comedies, variety shows, soaps, and music. Some comedians such as Bob Hope, Jack Benny, and Fred Allen became famous on the radio. Great comedies from the radio era included the *Amos 'n' Andy* show, *Fibber McGee and Molly*, and *George Burns and Gracie Allen*. They gained their fame on the radio. Many great band leaders such as Tommy Dorsey, Benny Goodman, and Glenn Miller brought music to the homes. My earliest favorite musicians were Liberace and Roger Williams. The men in our family liked the dramas such as *The Green Hornet*, *The Lone Ranger*, and *Superman*. Some of the popular soap operas were *Young Widow Brown* and *Ma Perkins*. These were listened to by moms and teenage daughters. Women looked forward to these fifteen-minute or thirty-minute shows.

Our battery-powered radio was a stand-alone unit that sat in a prominent corner of our living room. The cabinet, which held the radio, was about three feet tall, two feet wide, and probably eighteen inches in depth. It had a sleek brown wood finish. The battery that powered the unit was fairly large and looked somewhat like a car battery of today. Its size was approximately a foot long, eight to ten inches wide, and ten inches in height. These radios also had tubes with prongs. If there was a problem, it was not always the battery, but the tubes. An antenna was attached to the radio and the wire went out the window and was lifted upon a pole about twenty feet away from the house. I am not sure where the radio was purchased; however, I do know some things were ordered from a Sears and Roebuck catalog.

At our noon break from the fields, we always listened to "WIS News," then the "WIS Hired Hands." They sang real country music and were comical. DeWitt "Snuffy" Jenkins was their main leader and probably the biggest attraction when the group made personal appearances at schools and community events in the Midlands area. Ira Demery was another well-known singer and guitar player with the group. Pappy Sherrill sang with The Hired Hands for quite some time. This group had all stringed instruments at that time. "Snuffy" was their comedian and banjo player. Sometimes they would play a drum. I am unable to remember the names of the others.

My earliest memory of radio was the fireside chats of President F. D. Roosevelt. Even though I was very young at the time, I was aware that my parents were troubled. He held these events frequently in order to inform our nation about World War II. Some struggling farm families listened only the news reports. Many things were scarce because of war rationing during that period of time. Some were fearful of their battery going dead and not being able to purchase another one.

The first person in our family to get a television was my brother, Floyd. His black-and-white television was purchased in the mid-1950s. I remember he would watch boxing matches and other sports on his set. A new television was considered a luxury back then. My parents would think that we had come a long way with a television in most rooms.

PART 6

FARM LIFE

Chapter 15

FARMING FOR CASH AND CUISINE

Cotton Farming

IN MY EARLY years of growing up in Lexington County, most all farms grew cotton. Cotton farming is labor-intense farming. One needs to understand the seasons and the weather conditions, because it could make or break you.

Soon after the year's crop was picked in September and October, my dad and brothers ran over the stalks with a machine that cut them into pieces. During the winter they would plow the fields and, as Dad would say, "fallow the ground." If the soil appeared hard or lumpy, they would run a harrow over the fields to make it smooth. A harrow, from my time frame, was a heavy-framed piece of equipment with sharp-edged spikes drawn by a horse. It rooted up any weeds or roots and leveled the soil.

The soil sat idle for several months until just the right time. My dad, or Papa, as we called him, decided when the time had come by using the farmers' almanac or an educated guess. If the farmer planted too early, the frost could kill the crop and have to be replanted, which is costly. Should you plant too late, boll weevils would attack the bolls or pods that held the cotton. A boll weevil is a small grayish insect with a long beak. Its larvae hatches in cotton bolls. An attack destroys the young cotton growing inside.

The right timing meant everything to a small-time farmer, because each farmer wanted his first bale to get to the gin first in the fall. It seemed as if the earlier you sold the crop, the better price you received. After so much labor, everyone wanted all he could get per bale. Cotton farmers are not selfish but rather have survival instincts.

Usually in mid-March or early April, one of the men would run a shallow trench with a particular plow pulled by a horse over the entire field. This process is called "drawing the rows." The rows were thirty-two to thirty-four inches apart. A piece of equipment called the distributor dropped fertilizer in the trench and covered it, making a ridge. Another person would run the planter with special seed over the ridge made by the distributor and drop seeds. The planter had small blades or plow beams that would cover the seeds.

Our family bought seeds each year rather than save them from year to year. The younger children would fill a galvanized bucket with seeds for the planter or fertilizer for the distributor. There was never any gender bias in the Busbee household when it came to work. All the cultivation, fertilizing, and spraying was done with equipment pulled by horses. I can almost hear our men saying: "whoa," "gid up," "gee," or "haw." "Whoa" means stop, "gid up" means go forward, "gee" means go right, and "haw" means go left.

In about two weeks after planting the seeds, a new crop of seedlings usually began sprouting and growing. Then came the serious work for the older girls. We replanted seeds where there were gaps in the seedlings. After reseeding where necessary, we chopped the cotton plants. This process involved using a hoe and thinning out the plants where they were too close together to grow properly.

The guys cultivated the young plants by using a special plow blade to pull the soil toward plants. Any grass or weeds, which came up between the plants, were cut down or hoed by the girls. This process of cultivation and hoeing continued until sometime in June when the plants became too large for easy access. We already had gardens and other crops growing simultaneously.

Picking cotton was everybody's responsibility. I remember, quite well, my first cotton sack. My dad made it sound as if picking cotton was going to be fun. The cotton was quite pretty, but the brown bolls had sharp points that stuck our hands. Even for a five-year-old child, it did not take me long to figure out that plucking the fluffy white lint and putting it into a sack was not too much fun. Before the day got old, the back got tired. All of us worked as a unit. It was not all bad. The conversations and singing were fun for everyone.

The cotton "sack" was a burlap bag. A piece of cloth or burlap was folded several times to make a strap that fit over the user's shoulder, depending upon the individual's height. The strap was fastened to the sack by using a green cotton boll or another round object on each side of the sack and tying a knot around the strap and then the boll. Everyone had his own fitted sack.

At the end of the rows, we put out very large burlap sheets that we called "cotton sheets." Burlap is a coarse cloth made from jute or hemp, primarily used for making sacks. If I remember correctly, our sacks came originally with fertilizer in them. Each sheet was handmade from three fertilizer bags that were opened. Two bags were sewn together side-by-side and another was sewn lengthwise. (My youngest brother, Tracy, reminded me of this fact. His memory is better than mine.) The cotton sheets were spread out on the ground at the end of the rows. They had to be accessible by a wagon or trailer. A cotton scale looked somewhat like a tripod, made of poles with a metal measuring device using heavy bell-shaped weights, which hung down in the proper notches.

Each picker put the sack strap over his/ her shoulder, either left or right depending on which hand was preferred, left hand or right hand. Each of us pickers chose a row and started taking the white fluffy cotton from the open burrs held up by the stalks. Beginners are not very fast, but with a degree of patience, one can learn to use both hands pulling the white prize and shoving it into the sacks. Whenever the sack filled, it was dumped or emptied on a cotton sheet. This process continued all day long except for short water breaks and lunch during the middle of the day. After lunch that Mom prepared at home, we went back to the cotton patch. Near nightfall, the men tied up the sheets, weighed them, and put them on a wagon or trailer.

Often, after the family crop was picked and stored or sold, the older children would pick for nearby farmers to earn personal spending money. I remember picking for Mr. Jefferson, Mr. Laird, and Mr. Sid Smith, who owned Swansea Milling Company. Most of these big farmers gave us lunch and plenty of drinks.

At the end of every day the owners would weigh our individual sheets and keep a record until the end of the week. I remember, there were a few times I picked two hundred pounds in one day. The pay was one or two cents a pound, but that could amount to a lot for a kid. We usually bought clothes or anything special that we needed, such as extra school supplies or books.

The cotton we picked for my dad was stored under a shed until there was a big enough load to make a bale. Swansea area boasted of several cotton gins. Mr. Louie Rast and Mr. Wilkes owned the nearest to downtown. Several times I went with Dad to the gin. A big pipe came down over the wagon or the trailer and literally sucked it up. The ginning process took the seeds from the lint. Our cotton came out as a bale about five or six feet high by three or four feet in depth and width. The ginner would pay us for the seed. Then the bale of cotton was taken to the platform by the railroad tracks. The longer the staple was, the better the price. Buyers, such as the Riley brothers and several others, bid on the bales according to the grade. As shown in the picture, bales were left exposed on one side for grading purposes.

Some farmers preferred to take their seeds home and sell them later. Cotton seeds are used to make cottonseed oil, which in turn is used to produce cooking oil, margarine, soap, and etc. Cottonseed meal comes from the hulled cottonseed after the oil has been removed. It is used in fertilizer and fodder for the animals. The children liked to play in the seeds and thought nothing about the possibility of suffocation. It was especially dangerous before DDT, a powerful insecticide, was outlawed. Parents did not seem to sense the danger as we do today.

Cotton farming is a tough way to make a living. In good years, the money was good, but in bad seasons it could spell disaster to a family eking out a living. Cotton was an important part of my childhood, as it was with most Lexington County country families.

Watermelons for Cash

Watermelon farming is much simpler and less labor intensive than cotton. The watermelon crop, which the Busbee farm raised for cash, was usually planted after the grain crops, such as oats or wheat, were harvested. A watermelon is a large, round or oblong fruit with a hard, green rind and juicy pink, red, or yellow pulp with many seeds.

Our crop was usually planted in early June. This time frame was chosen because of the short growing season of sixty to ninety days. Dad chose August as the right time to market his produce, thereby avoiding the larger farms and the Florida crops, which were ripe in the spring and early summer. The return on his investment seemed to be much better with the later ripening season. The August crop also missed the rush on our summer gardens and the corn crop.

After the early crop was harvested, usually in early May, the field of five to ten acres was disked or plowed with special plow beams. Sometimes my dad would spread manure from the chicken pens, cow stall, or the horse stables before turning the soil. This was not always the case. Nevertheless, he made sure the field was level and free of lumps or clods of soil. Watermelons seem to grow better in light, sandy soils than in clay soil. Now was the time to "draw the rows." The rows for watermelons were much farther apart than for most crops other than cantaloupes. One of the men would run a shallow trench with a particular plow, pulled by a horse, over the entire field at least five feet apart. The distance of the rows was necessary due to the vigorous growth of the watermelon vines, which produce the prized fruit. When the field had not been fertilized earlier with animal manure, the distributor with a complete fertilizer dropped the fertilizer in the trench and covered it, making a small ridge or mound. Here again, a younger child would fill the galvanized bucket with fertilizer and keep the distributor filled. Most of the commercial fertilizer was purchased from the Riley Brothers' business in Swansea. Occasionally Dad would buy in Columbia from one of the many feed and seed stores, which were plentiful in the 1940s and 1950s. Several of these stores were off Gervais and Wayne Streets. This part of Columbia is now called the Vista.

Unlike cotton seeds, which were purchased yearly, we often saved watermelon seeds from year to year. Several seeds were dropped into holes dug five feet apart, made by using a hoe on the mound made by the distributor. For marketing purposes, we grew Garrisons, which are long melons with dark green and white or cream stripes running the entire length of the watermelon. Its fruit is a lovely shade of red and tasty. Sometimes we planted Black Diamonds (Cannon Ball) melons that are round with a deep green color. The Black Diamond required a longer growing season of sixty to ninety days.

Once the seedlings were growing, the cultivating began, which is less intense than other crops. The men cultivated the young plants by taking a special plow blade to pull the soil toward the plants. When the vines started growing, one of the younger children would turn the vines, so that the plow could get the fresh soil near the base of the plants. As soon as the plant began growing long vines, the plowing ceased. We could just watch them grow, and grow they did, in our hot and humid weather. Most commercial watermelon crops are grown in the South, where our growing season is longer and hotter. The Garrison watermelons grew to twenty or thirty inches long or longer. They could easily weigh forty to fifty pounds or more. The Black Diamond (Cannon Ball) was perfectly round and weighed forty or fifty-plus pounds. Each watermelon plant could produce ten or more watermelons.

It takes experience to determine when a watermelon is ripe; a novice can't do it. The skin color does not change at maturity as the cantaloupe does. The test that we used was based on sound. The ripe melon's sound is a muffled or a dead sound indicating ripeness. A metallic sound indicates lack of maturity. This test is very dependable to a person who is an experienced thumper. Sometimes Dad would stand the melon on its end. His expertise taught him that a slight color change on the bottom of the melon from white to cream meant that the melon was ripe. Often my dad would cut a melon open to show his prospective buyers the beautiful meat of our watermelons. Most of the melons within the field ripened within a week or so of each other.

Sale of the crop is the real challenge. Many times our dad would try to sell the entire field of watermelons to a wholesale distributor or a trucking firm out of Columbia. If someone offered Dad a "reasonable or fair" price, he would usually sell immediately. However, if a good offer was not made, we picked the watermelons and loaded them on a trailer that he pulled behind his old Ford car. Carrying the heavy "fruit of our labor" is hot and sweaty work. I have helped load many melons for the State Farmers' Market. Back in the 1940s and early 1950s, the Farmers' Market was on Assembly Street in Columbia. Vendors were in the center of the wide street before the cement medians were built. I even remember a water fountain for horses that was near the downtown post office at the intersection of Assembly and Taylor Streets. Most of the time, Dad would find a buyer for his entire load, but not always. If he did not get a quick sale, he sold them piecemeal style, sometimes staying late into the night.

I believe watermelon farming was the best paying crop for the overhead and the labor put into the crop. The only downside to watermelon farming was the fact that young people would steal them from our field. Their stealing was a real issue to our parents. Until this day, I enjoy seeing them grow and eating them. Fond memories flood my mind of swimming in Bull Swamp and eating cold watermelons.

Turnips and Mustard Greens - Cash Crop

The turnip is a fast-growing, cool weather vegetable. The turnip belongs to the mustard branch of the cabbage family. This family of vegetables also includes rutabaga. No one knows how long turnips have been eaten. They were commonly eaten by the Greeks and the Romans. History tells us that turnips were a favorite food in England and northern Europe. Farmers have grown them since colonial times in the United States.

Turnip roots and greens are a wonderful food and are rich in vitamins A, B complex, and C. They give a lot of flavor to the diet and bulk that regulates the body. The mustard greens are also rich in vitamins and minerals needed by the human body.

The Busbee farm grew turnips and mustard greens for home use and as a cash crop. We grew the purple-top turnip and the curly-top mustard greens for the market. My dad liked to clear a new ground patch for his marketing turnip crop. Turnips deplete the soil of its nutrients quickly. They need to be rotated annually in order to avoid the depletion of the soil. Many times in August, Dad would slash the small saplings and undergrowth from an area no larger than an acre. Then the larger stumps would be pulled up manually. Next, someone would run over the area with a disk type plow. Any loose roots and/or rocks would be removed from the chosen area by hand and piled outside the area. Removing the debris was tiring and dirty work. After the roots and rocks were removed, the men would level the area with the harrower.

The guys would spread manure from the stables or cow stall over the entire area.

The fall crop would be sown in about sixty days, mid to late August, before the first expected frost. We aimed for the latter part of October. The turnip seeds and mustard seeds were sown in different areas of the newly cleared plot. The seeds were raked under the soil ever so slightly. Once the seeds were sown, there was no more work unless the aphids attacked the greens. Should there be an aphid attack, the plants could be dusted or sprayed with a sulfate powder. If all went as expected, we could just sit back and wait for them to grow.

During the latter part of October, the crop would be ready for harvest. Here again, this was a family project. There was a small branch, or rill, with four or five inches of water, which ran through the woods between our barns and the fields. The men would pull the turnips from the ground and fill a wagon or trailer. Then they would bring the load of turnips to the stream of water for the younger children to wash. Remember, by the end of October, the weather was getting chilly. My sister Lois, younger brother Hosea, and I would dip the purple-topped root into the cold water and clean them well. We made sure there was no dirt left on them. With a rubber band or small cord, we tied together six to eight turnips to make a market-sized bunch. We went through this routine until the entire load was clean and ready to market. The mustard greens were bunched for market similarly, but the roots were cut off. The mustard roots are not tubers like the turnip root. I can't remember having to wash the mustard greens. The children's work was finished. Now Dad was responsible for selling them. Occasionally, one of us would go to the State Farmers' Market with him.

The turnip crop was a good cash crop. It offered a good return on the investment. Because both the roots and the greens are eaten, the southern states use a lot of them. Turnips, mustard, and collards are my favorite vegetables. We did not plant collards for cash, only for the family to eat.

Soybeans for Cash

The soybean plant is an annual that belongs to the pea family and is often called a legume. Soybeans were grown in China five thousand years ago for medical use. The plant has been grown in the United States for about 175 years. In the early years, it was planted for hay and livestock feed. Later, it was planted for the bean itself. The soybean is an excellent source of vegetable oil and protein.

On the Busbee farm, soybeans were planted after an early crop was harvested. After the wheat or oats crop was harvested in May or early

June, the field was plowed with a disk, which would turn under any stalks or shafts that were left on the ground. The plant materials left on the ground added nutrients to the soil. Our soybean crop was planted in late June or early July with an expected harvest in September or October.

My dad or one of my brothers would draw the rows. The rows were about three feet apart. A distributor with fertilizer dropped the fertilizer in the trench and covered it, making a ridge. Another person would run the planter with the seeds over the ridge made by the distributor and drop the seeds. The planter had small blades that would cover the seeds. One of the younger children would keep the distributor filled with fertilizer and the planter filled with seeds. This process continued until the whole field was planted.

In a week to ten days, the seeds should have sprouted and the plants visible. The men cultivated the young plants with a special plow blade to pull the soil toward the plants. Any grass or weeds that came up between the plants, the girls cut down with a hoe. The cultivation continued until the plants became too large for easy access. At that point, we just let them grow.

The plant grows from two to three-and-a-half feet or more in height. The stems, leaves, and pods are covered with short, fine brown or gray hairs. Small purple or white flowers appear where the leaf joins the stems. The pod or hull contains two to four round or oval seeds (beans). The beans themselves may be colored a shade of yellow, brown, or black, or possibly speckled. If my memory serves me well, ours were usually brown.

The characteristics of both the plant and the bean vary with the soil, cultivation, and seasonal conditions. Soybeans grow best in areas where corn grows well. They need soil that contains the nitrogen-fixing organism, which can produce nodules on the plant's roots. The crop yield is less without this soil feature. The chemistry of the soybean plant enriches the soil for other crops that follow them.

Once the soybeans are ready to harvest, our family would hire someone with a combine to harvest the crop. It would be painstaking to gather them by hand, because of the hairy feature on the stalks and pods. The combine bagged the beans. They were usually sold to a wholesale dealer.

Soybeans are a good cash crop with a good return on investment and labor. The United States' largest single source of vegetable oil and protein meal for livestock feeding comes from the soybean. Its many uses make it a very viable plant.

Corn Farming

Corn is probably the most valuable crop grown in the United States. It is ranked along with wheat, rice, and potatoes as the four most important crops in the world. The men on the ship with Christopher Columbus discovered corn in 1492. This was the first time white men had heard of the plant that we call corn. The people in the British Isles called corn *maize* (indigenous corn). Maize is another word for yellow. Our family planted corn for livestock feed and for the family to eat fresh or dried.

Throughout North and South America, corn is a favorite food. It is eaten as corn on the cob, hominy or grits, corn flakes, and popcorn. South Americans eat many foods made from corn, including tamales and tortillas. Corn is grown in almost every state in the United States. Historically the United States produces about 50 percent of all corn grown in the world. Four-fifths of the corn grown on farms in the United States is fed to livestock. The Busbee farm was not much different. Our family fed corn to our horses, cow, hogs, and chickens. Not only did we harvest the corn ears but also the cornstalks for livestock feed. In August, after the corn was ripe, we pulled the fodder or cut the stalks and put them in bundles. This was hot and sweaty work.

As soon as a crop was harvested, my dad and/or brothers would plow the field. Any time the ground seemed too hard or lumpy, they would run a harrow over the field to make it smooth. The harrow got rid of any weeds or roots and leveled the soil. About the middle of March, one of the men would make a shallow trench with a horse-pulled plow over the entire field where the corn was to be planted. The rows were about three feet apart.

One of the younger children would drop the kernels of corn, one by one, ahead of the person handling the distributor, which dropped the fertilizer in the trench and covered it, forming a ridge. The distributor blades would cover the seeds. The seeds that we used were from our barn. We picked the largest ears and shucked and shelled the ears of corn. Usually, two of the children would be kept from school to help with the corn planting. One child would drop the seeds and another would keep the distributor filled with fertilizer. The fertilizer was bought from a local dealer, Riley Brothers, or from a Columbia feed and seed store. Mid-March was planting time.

Within ten days to two weeks, the seedlings would be up. Should gaps appear in the rows, grains of corn would be dug in the missing spots. We did the replanting with a regular garden hoe. Crows seemed to like our cornfields and would pull the new plants for the grains of corn. Sometimes we would build scarecrows in the fields to frighten away the crows or blackbirds. A scarecrow is simple to make and a bit of fun. They were made from our old worn-out clothes and stuffed with straw or hay.

The corn plant is actually an unusual type of grass. The group of true grains or cereals include corn, wheat, barley, oats, rice, and rye. Usually, the corn plant grows three to ten feet tall and has many short branches called ear shoots. The stalk is a tough cornstalk or stem. The center of the stalk is a core of pith, which is a soft, spongy tissue. The plant's root system is complex with prop roots growing out of the stalk above the ground. These upper roots support the plant against wind. The tassel grows at the top of the cornstalk and contains hundreds of small flowers that produce pollen. Pink is the most common color of the tassel but it may be white, yellow, green, or red.

The ears of corn grow from the places where the leaves join the stalk. A corn plant may have one ear or as many as eight. In my early years on the farm, ours grew two or three ears of corn. Each ear has a corncob covered with rows of kernels. Each ear has an even row of kernels ranging from eight to twelve rows. There are at least six different types of corn that have different kinds of kernels. There is dent corn, sweet corn, flint corn, popcorn, flour corn, and pod corn. Dent corn and flint corn are what we commonly call field corn. These varieties are fed to animals; however, field corn can be eaten by humans as in our family's case.

Sweet corn is grown mainly for people to eat. My dad grew both kinds, but sweet corn was grown in a garden area on a much smaller scale. Most corn grown in the United States for commercial use is dent corn. It is called dent corn because each kernel or grain has a small dent on its top. Dent corn is usually harvested when the seeds become hard and dry. Sweet corn must be picked at just the right time to be sure that the taste is at its best. Sweet corn should be picked when the milky fluid fills the kernels. It is not good if left until the kernels start to get hard. One reason we did not grow much sweet corn was because it must be refrigerated quickly or it loses its flavor after being harvested. Therefore, much of the corn that was canned by our family was dent corn rather than sweet corn. Most of the sweet corn that we grew was eaten as corn on the cob. It is so sweet and has a wonderful flavor and is a great source of vitamins A and C. Also the sugar content is a good source of energy.

Our family seldom grew popcorn because it is a "fun food." It has small, hard kernels with pointed round ends. There is a tough outer coat on each kernel. When heated rapidly, the moisture inside turns to steam and causes the kernel to burst and its entire inside puffs out. Other kinds of corn crack and parch but will not pop. We fed corn to our horses, cows, hogs, and chickens. Cornmeal and grits were ground from our corn. Our large family ate many bushels as fresh corn or as canned soup with tomatoes and okra or as succotash. It is a great survival food.

Wheat and Oats Farming

The most important grains in the world markets are wheat, corn, rice, barley, oats, sorghum, millet, and rye. Wheat and oats are among man's most important food crops. They belong to the grass family and are referred to as cereals or cereal grains. Because of their high starch content, it makes them an excellent source of energy for man and animals. The common term, grain, actually refers to the seed produced by the cereals. In the United States, corn and wheat occupy the largest acreage.

Grain has two chief purposes: food for mankind and food for livestock. Unlike corn that is eaten by simply cooking it, other grains must be processed.

As soon as the summer crops were harvested, corn or soybeans, the stalks were chopped down and plowed under. A large field could take several days to till it well. Any clots or hard lumps were broken up by pulling a harrow over the field. My dad liked a well-cultivated look to his fields. Once the field was turned well, fertilizer was spread over the empty field before the harrowing occurred. The plowing of the field to plant grain usually occurred in late October or early November. Cereal grains are winter crops. Dad or an older brother spread the wheat seed manually over the field. The harrow covered the seeds and fertilized at the same time. Once the wheat seeds were planted, the wheat was left to grow all winter. In early spring the wheat plants grow a stem with a head that bears a shaft. The shaft holds the golden grains. When the grains become dry, they are ready to be harvested. Our family did not own a combine; therefore, we made arrangements with a farmer who owned one. The combine would go over the entire field, plucking the golden grain. The shaft was blown away in the harvesting process. Our golden wheat was bagged in burlap bags for storage.

The bags of wheat were stored in a barn until the family needed fresh-ground flour.

The wheat grains stored from the farm were ground into flour at a milling company. There were two places in the vicinity that ground wheat, Poole's Mill on Highway #3 and Adluh Flour in Columbia. The ground flour was stored in large bags, which held fifty pounds. The family used the flour to make bread and other baked goods. The fresh ground flour had no additives, not even salt, baking soda, or baking powder.

The stalks, after the grain was harvested, were hewed down and raked into piles, and were fed to the horses and cows. It could be made into large stacks or stored in the hayloft in the main barn.

Oats belong to the same grass family as wheat and are planted almost identically to the wheat crop. The oats crop was not placed close to the wheat to avoid cross-pollination. Oats and wheat are planted in the autumn. They are usually harvested in late April or early May.

Unlike the wheat harvest, many times my dad would cut the oats with his horse-drawn mower as if it were hay. After the grain was cut, the hay rake was run over the entire field, making piles of oats. The oats could be stacked as haystacks for several months or stored in the hayloft in the largest barn.

Farmers in the U.S. use great percentages of the corn, oats, sorghum, and barley as food for the livestock. Indirectly, we ate a large share of the grain fed to our animals. We drank the milk from our cows and ate the meat and eggs and other foods produced by those animals. By far, our country consumes indirectly more grains than almost any other country, because they do not have enough food to feed grain to animals.

A large number of other products are derived from grains. Alcoholic beverages are made by fermentation of grain. Many industrial products contain grain as a by-product, such as starch used in paper and fabrics. Starch is used in making drugs, cosmetics, explosives, and paste. Some grains contain chemicals used in making plastics and certain petroleum products. The fact that our family used our oats for animal food does not mean all farmers use their oats to feed their animals. However, in our immediate area, oats were fed to the animals.

Peanuts

Our family farm grew peanuts on a limited scale. Many of our neighbors were like us in that they planted peanuts for their family's use only. In the general area, some farmers planted them on a large scale as a cash crop. South and east of Swansea, in Orangeburg and Calhoun counties, peanut farming was more prevalent in my youth than today. Growing peanuts is labor-intensive farming unless you are equipped with much more modern equipment than we ever owned.

Most people think that a peanut is a nut, but it is a type of pea instead. It is similar to peas in that it grows seed in a pod or shell. Each pod (shell) contains at least two peanuts. It is possible to have only one peanut in a shell, but it can have as many as five peanuts.

The thing that makes peanuts unique is that its pods or shells grow underground. Peanuts are sometimes called groundnuts or goobers. Some mischievous children are sometimes called slow thinkers, "Goober heads." My take on the name calling is that peanuts are small and the victim child is being referred to as having a small brain.

Our peanuts were planted in a small area similar to a garden crop. They are planted somewhat like soybeans. Peanuts like well-drained soil that has been plowed deeply so the soil remains loose around the roots. The rows are about thirty to thirty-six inches apart. The seeds are planted two or three inches deep and about a foot apart. The soil needs to be cultivated often to keep it loose. Grass and weeds must be removed from between the plants.

Peanuts must have plenty of sunshine, a moderate rainfall, and a long growing time. Normally, it takes about four months from planting the seed until the crop can be harvested. The peanut plant grows upward of two-and-a-half feet high. The bunch type spreads outward as much as three to four feet across. The plant has many small pea-like flowers, which open at sunrise. Then the flowers wither and fall off. Their cycle is amazing. The blooms grow where the leaves are attached to the stems. The blossoming season is quite long; they blossom continuously for two to three months. The buds open at sunrise, and strangely fertilization takes place during the morning and the bloom normally withers and dies about noon. In a few days at the point where the blossom grows, the pegs (stalk-like stems of the pods) begin to grow. Slowly these pegs grow downward at first but start to grow more quickly.

The pegs grow down into the soil to a depth of one to three inches. Sometimes the tentacle-like peg may grow as much as seven inches below the ground's surface. The tip of the peg contains the developing peanut. The tips swell and develop into the pods that contain the peanuts.

Harvesting the crop at exactly the right time is critical. The timing is so important, because if they are plowed up too soon, the pods will not be filled or ripened. Should they be left too long, the pegs, tentacle-like roots, could snap off. This would leave a lot of the entire pod crop in the ground. The way we harvested the peanuts was simple, but very time-consuming. One of our men would run a special plow down the middle of the row to slice through the main root of the plants below ground level. The plants with the pods would be lifted from the dirt and left to dry in the sun. The peanuts were plucked from the plant by hand and put in buckets or baskets. Matured or green peanuts would be picked from the plant as soon as it is uprooted, if they were going to be boiled. Otherwise, they needed to be dried before storage for any length of time.

Our family liked to boil them in salt water for a tasty treat. The dried ones were roasted in the oven. The old timers in my generation called them parched. Most people from the South like to snack on peanuts, which is a healthy food. One reason we did not grow peanuts often was that they were always accessible in downtown Swansea. We even had our own peanut expert. Mr. Everett Furtick was called "Mr. Peanut Furtick." Mr. Peanut grew his peanuts in the country. He boiled and roasted them and brought them to downtown Swansea's Main Street to sell on Saturdays. This is how he made a living. I am not sure what made his peanuts so delicious, but they were known in the 1940s and early 1950s as the best around.

The farmers of large farms who raise peanuts as a cash crop need to have the proper equipment to grow them. Modern farmers have combines that dig up the plant. Usually, they are dug up from the soil then left to dry for a few days. The combines pick up the plants and strip the nuts from the plants and place the picked pods in a collection bin. These nuts are dried completely and graded for the markets. Sometimes they are picked half-dried and dried artificially.

Most of the peanuts grown in the U.S. are used as food. There is more energy and calories in roasted peanuts or peanut butter than beefsteak weighing the same. Nearly half of the peanuts consumed in the United States are made into peanut butter. A quarter of the nuts are sold as roasted peanuts. They are used in candies, cookies, pies and pastries. Some ice cream is flavored with peanut butter.

In South Georgia, there are peanut factories. These manufacturers use presses to dissolve the oil from the nuts. Peanut oil is used for frying food. Other edible products are made from this oil, including salad dressings, margarine, and vegetable oils.

The lower grades of peanut oil are used to grease machinery, make soaps, face powder, shaving cream, and shampoos. Some paints contain peanut oil. Nitroglycerin, an explosive, contains peanut oil. Even the shells are used in the manufacturing of plastics, artificial corks, and wallboards. The plants make good hay but most farmers return the plants to the farms because the plants fertilize the soil.

Inside Farmers' Cotton Gin
Left to right: Marvin Rish, manager of gin,
John Henry Dowd, Furman Saylor, farmers;
E. Fulton Hoover, SHS Agriculture teacher.
(Used by permission Mrs. Melba Hoover)

Cultivated field ready to plant

Field of growing peanuts, photo by Loretta Hutto

Field of peanuts ready for harvest, photo by Loretta Hutto

Chapter 16

Tools of the Trade

MANUAL FARMING REQUIRES real hard work. This lifestyle is not for lazy people. Everyone in the Busbee family had responsibilities. Dad really believed in the old adage, "If you don't work, you don't eat." Our workday was long, sunup to sundown. Farming is composed of a number of phases—harnessing the animals, plowing, cultivating, fertilizing, weeding, and harvesting.

Manual farmers, like my dad, have a genuine relationship with their horses. Only farmers can understand this concept, those who have worked with horses day by day, year after year, and watched the devotion to the master. There was never a doubt our horses loved my dad and my brothers. My dad's horses were his most prized tool! His horses possessed an untiring and eager willingness to work and sweat at Dad's bidding. All they got in return was feed, water, and a pat on the back. The horses nuzzled their drivers as they rested in the shade at the end of a lengthy row of cotton or corn. Personal attention, almost as much as the farmer gave his children, was required to keep a horse in top shape. A little rock or stone in the horse's foot could disable the horse for days or months. Not having his horse could spell disaster for the farmer.

The harness was about as important as the horse. Harnessing a horse was a daily chore; it was a skill that was not lost in history. A harness was made up of many parts: the hames, the collar, the traces, the crupper, tongue chains, breeching, collar pads, bellyband, reins, bits, blinders, and neck strap. The harness was made of cowhide, riveted and sewn together for durability and strength.

A harness is the leather straps and metal pieces by which a horse or mule is fastened to a buggy, wagon, plow, or other load. The bridle is the headpiece that goes over the animal's ears and under its chin or neck. It consists of the headstall, bit, and reins. The main straps hold two metal circles near the mouth. Attached to these metal circles are the bits in the horse's mouth. This is where the phrase "chomping at the bit" came from. The bits' purpose is the guiding tool for obedience. Long ropes, called the reins, are attached to the circles on each side of the horse's head. My brothers and Dad used the reins to control the animal. Another set of straps goes over the back and under the belly. The belly straps or bellyband hold the wagon or plow tongue in place. Last, but not least, heavy chains or traces are attached to the collar's hames and belly straps and then to the single or double tree, which is a long wooden bar across the wagon or other farm instrument. The hames are two rigid pieces along the sides of a collar to which the traces are attached. Most harnesses have a breeching, which is a strap around the hindquarters to help the horse hold back on a downgrade. This strap prevents the wagon from hitting the horse.

Each morning before harnessing the animals, they must be fed and curried. A currycomb is a metal brush that we used daily to keep the horses' hair shiny and healthy. Our horses were brushed every day before beginning the work cycle. Dad and/or my brothers checked the horses' feet regularly to be sure the shoes were on properly. The horseshoes were nailed to the hooves and protect the tender portion of the soles of the feet.

The harness for a workhorse is very heavy and cumbersome. To get it on and off the horse and hung in proper order requires skill (not a little trick). It has to be hung in proper order on a peg in the stable or barn wall. The Busbee men had stamina and were strong for their size. Every farm, regardless of size, needs special tools for each phase: plowing, fertilizing, cultivating, weeding, harvesting, and threshing.

(1) *Plowing* is the process of turning over and breaking up the soil. The disk plow is used to turn up the soil. After the soil is broken up, a harrow is used to smooth the soil and get rid of rocks and other debris. A spike-tooth harrow has a heavy frame with spikes drawn by a horse or mule. We used it for breaking up and leveling the plowed ground. The disk harrow has sharp and circular blades used to break up the soil for sowing seeds, such as wheat or oats. When we broke new ground or cleared an area of trees and brush, first the soil was tilled or plowed several times, then a harrow went over the area many times. This process helped us to rid the area of roots and other trash. If the debris is not removed, it is almost impossible to use the plow that pushes the soil around the plants. Our farm owned several different kinds of plows. The various plow parts were attached to the plow stock according to need.

1. Middle Buster – This plow was used for digging potatoes and to make corn rows.

2. Row opening plow – This plow was used to make garden rows.

3. Row scrape – This plow was used to plow corn, cotton, and gardens.

4. Drawing plow point – This tool was used to draw various rows for crops.

5. Middle buster point – This tool was used for deep plowing.

6. Turn plow blade – This blade was used on a jig plow for row crops.

7. Supplemental plow blade – Extra blade.

(2) *Fertilizing* is mixing plant food and/or manure into the soil to help plants grow. Like people, plants must be fed in order to grow. We fertilized them for growth. My family used a distributor to spread the fertilizer in the previously drawn rows. A distributor has a wooden frame somewhat like the plow stock with a metal wheel on the bottom center. A large bucket, with controls in the center of the bottom, rests on the wooden frame and is attached with metal bolts. There is a control lever on the upper rim of the bucket that opens and closes the slot on the underside. The distributor drops plant food in the rows when the slot in the bottom of the bucket is opened by the control lever. The fertilizer used in the distributor was purchased from a feed and seed store or from a dealer in Swansea who sold plants, farm gadgets, and bagged fertilizer.

We also used chicken, cow, and horse manure as fertilizer. Each time the stables or chicken coops were cleaned, the manure was spread in the fields. A wagon or wheelbarrow was loaded with manure and hauled to a field or garden plot. The manure was spread with pitchforks and shovels. Our men did this task, which was slow and heavy labor.

(3) *Cultivating* means keeping the soil loose around plants. To cultivate means to stir up the soil around the growing plants. Several tools were used in the cultivation of our fields. A sweep plow was used to pull soil up to the young plants. A sweep is a blade of plow point of various widths used in shallow cultivation or row crops. We also had a cultivator, which is a machine used in loosening the earth and destroying weeds around the growing plants. My family used the cultivator with crops such as corn or cotton.

The standard hoe was one of the most important tools on our farm. The hoe is a tool with a thin flat blade set across the end of a long handle used for weeding and loosening the soil. The types of hoes are nursery, weeding, gardening, and serrated. All of the girls in our family were all too familiar with hoes. We chopped cotton, took weeds from the corn crop, and hoed the vegetable garden. Chopping cotton is the process of thinning the plantlets where there were too many plants in a hill. The girls used the hoes and the boys used the plow!

(4) *Harvesting* his crop is the most joyful time of a farmer's life—it is his pay day! Harvesting is the job of gathering the harvest or crop. My family used many tools in the process of gathering our crops. The scythe is a tool with a long single-edge blade set at an angle with a long handle, while the sickle is similar with a short handle. Both of these tools are used for cutting long grass or grain by hand. Before my dad owned a hay cutter or mower, he cut oats with a scythe and bundled them. Once he was able to get a mower and a hay rake, gathering grain and hay was much easier.

(5) *Threshing* is the process of separating stems and husks from grain or seeds. On our farm we used this process on our wheat and oats, but mostly the wheat. Usually, Dad arranged to get someone who owned a combine to harvest the wheat. A combine is a power-operated harvesting machine that cuts, threshes, and cleans the grain at the same time.

In gathering wood used for cooking and heating, we used several tools: an axe, saws, and wedges. The most common tool for cutting wood was the cross-cut saw. This saw was about six feet long with a thin metal blade with notched edge teeth, which had irregular spaced notches set in a perfect pattern. On each end of the thin blade were round pegs about twelve to eighteen inches long. The cutting process required two people with near equal strength who could pull the handles back and forth to cut the log into pieces. When the log was fairly small, we chopped it with an axe. Once the pieces of wood were cut, we sometimes used a wedge to split the log into small pieces. A wedge is a piece of hard material, like wood or metal, tapering from a thick back to a thin edge that can be driven or forced into a narrow opening to split the wood. Wooden wedges are used to reinforce a structure. We always needed nails and tacks for many different tasks. Nails were purchased in wooden kegs because that way they were much cheaper.

Illustration of horse bridle

Horse collar

Double horse wagon, photo by Linda Shealy

Chapter 17

FOOD FROM THE BARNYARD

Chickens

THE CHICKEN WAS a common farm bird and probably the most versatile creature on our family farm. We raised them for the edible eggs and for meat; therefore, the female (hen) and the male (rooster) were important to us. Our family raised several types of chickens, such as Rhode Island Reds, Plymouth Rock, and Dominique. The Rhode Island Red is a breed of American chicken with reddish-brown feathers and a black tail. The Plymouth Rock ranges in color from white to gray with darker stripes. The Dominique is a domestic breed with yellow legs and gray barred plumage. I remember ours being gray-and-white checkered.

Housing for the chickens was called a chicken coop. Our chicken coop was a building approximately eight feet by ten feet and about eight feet high. It was constructed of rough wood nailed to corner posts, which were anchored in the ground. The roof was made of tin. It had a homemade door made from unfinished lumber on crude hinges, about two feet wide and six feet high. Wooden slats were attached to walls the width of the structure beginning near ground-level and going almost to the ceiling. The slats closest to the ground were in the back and the highest ones were near the entry. The chickens always came back into the coop in the late evening to roost on the slats. It is fascinating to see these big birds asleep, crouched on a wooden slat. We always locked the entry door at night to keep foxes or other varmints out.

On the top sides of the chicken coop were rows of covered box-like bins filled with straw. Here is where the hens laid their eggs. One of my chores was to gather the eggs from the bins in the late afternoon. On one occasion gathering eggs, I found a black snake in the nest. It scared me badly, but no harm was done. Sometimes, a setting hen on the nest would give me some bad pecks. This is where the phrase "mad as a setting hen" originated. Often, Mom would return twelve to fifteen eggs to the nest when she realized the hen wanted to set. That hen sat on those eggs for three weeks until the eggs were incubated or hatched. The hen left the nest only briefly to get food. After the chicks or biddies hatched, the mother hen and her babies were put in a separate pen for several weeks.

The eggs from the chicken coop were our breakfast food. Our family could eat a dozen eggs at one meal. Extra eggs, not needed in the kitchen, were sold or traded for other grocery items not grown on the farm, such as sugar, shortening, and flour. Within six or eight weeks, we were able to determine which ones were roosters. The young roosters were destined for the frying pan. Only a few avoided the destiny of the other fryers. We never kept many roosters, because they would fight about the hens. Fried chicken was the Sunday special or saved until guests were expected.

Let me explain the process of the chosen rooster from the chicken yard to the dining table. One of my brothers would use a long wire with a hook on the end and walk in the midst of the chickens, hooking the desired rooster around its leg. Once this task was accomplished, he would walk away with his catch to a more secluded place and wring the chicken's neck. The chicken would flop on the ground a few minutes; then its neck was cut off to let the blood drain from its flesh. A bucket of hot water was ready, and the dead chicken was immersed in the hot water for a short time. Hot water loosened the feathers so they could be plucked from the flesh. It takes only a few minutes to clear all the feathers. The next step was to open it up and remove the insides and discard everything but the liver and gizzard (craw). This task was usually done the day before we expected to eat the chicken. Usually, it was done in late evening, because chickens go to roost just before dark.

We would eat the older hens one by one as they aged. We made delicious chicken and dumplings, chicken salad, and sometimes, we roasted or baked them and made corn bread dressing as we did with turkeys. I like chicken anyway it is cooked. Tracy says he can still smell the wet feathers. Needless to say, he doesn't like chicken.

The chickens were fed corn, which was grown on the farm, and the young chicks were fed chicken feed sold in the feed and seed stores. Their water came from the manual pump. After the family meal, any leftover green leafy vegetables were fed to the chickens. The manure from the chicken coop was spread over the ground in a field. This is a good grade fertilizer and cut the cost of commercial fertilizer considerably.

Raising chickens is a cycle. If we killed too many during the winter, Mom would sometimes buy baby chicks in the spring from a breeder in quantities of twenty-five to a hundred chicks. That way, we always had young chickens for cooking and hens for laying eggs. The worst enemy of a chicken is the hawk. I remember the noise whenever a hawk flew over the farm. It is quite fascinating to watch the mother hen clucking for the biddies when she sensed danger. The hen would squat on the ground and cover the chicks under her body and wings. The scripture in Matthew 23:37 compares the hen's love of her babies to how Christ desires to protect his people if they would only heed his warning. Instinct caused the little chicks to rush to the hen for protection. Obedience to the Word should teach us to seek the favor of the Lord.

Hogs and Pigs

A pig is a domesticated animal with a long, broad snout and a thick, fat body covered with course bristles of hair. The young animal is referred to as a pig until it weighs at least 100 pounds. At that point he/she is considered a hog. The female hog is called a sow and the male is a boar. Both are used for meat. On our farm the young hogs were sometimes called shoats. A shoat is a medium-sized animal.

Approximately a fourth of the meat eaten in the United States is pork. Our family raised hogs for ham, bacon, fatback, sausage, liver pudding, and pork chops. Some of the lard we used came from the hogs. The meat left after the fat has been taken out is called cracklings. Cracklings were cooked in cornmeal and called crackling cornbread. It was cooked as a loaf/pone or as corn muffins. My parents also made lye soap with fat from the hogs. We occasionally ate pork rinds.

Most farming countries raise hogs. About one-third of the farms in the United States raise hogs for their meat and by-products. The regions of the country where corn is a main crop, hog farming became concentrated as a profitable business. There are quite a number of hog farms in North Carolina and South Carolina.

Our hogs were raised in a sty or hog pen. Many people think of hogs as dirty and dull/stupid because they wallow in the mud. In reality, they are neither dirty nor stupid. They are cleaner than many other animals. We fed our hogs corn grown on the farm and slop (table scraps) from the kitchen. They also ate watermelon and cantaloupe rinds. Hogs enjoy the peelings and cores from apples or pears. Our hogs were fed twice a day.

Butchering the hogs was done in the winter when it was very cold. Both parents, older children, and our black neighbor Abraham Sutton and sometimes Jack Hall would help with butchering. That day was always a long and hard day's work. Early in the morning, one of the men would shoot the chosen hog with a rifle and then the hog's throat was slashed to let the blood run. This prevented the meat from being bloody. Once the hog was dead and ready, it was hoisted up on a tree limb or pole. A large pot or vat of scalding hot water was waiting. The animal was dipped in the water until the hair would come off the body easily. The men would use knives to scrape off the hair. The skin must be clean and hairless. The head was removed from the body to be cleaned later in the day. While still hanging, the center of the hog's belly was opened up. All the organs and the intestines were removed. Almost everything was used.

The ladies had their share of chores. In our big iron washpot, the liver and other organs were cooked. Someone cooked a large pot of rice on the kitchen stove for the liver pudding. Some of the older kids cleaned the intestines to be used as casings for the sausage and the liver pudding. This was never my chosen thing to do because they smell bad. The casings could be bought in the grocery store if help was limited. We had a meat grinder that was bolted to an outdoor table. Certain parts of the meat were ground for sausage.

Our family mixed sage, onion, and garlic, along with salt and red pepper in the sausage. The sausage mixture was stuffed into the casing. Once the liver and other parts were cooked well and ground, it was mixed with the cooked rice, along with onions, salt, and pepper. This, too, was stuffed in the larger casings. Not much was wasted in the butchering process. My dad liked the brain cooked with eggs, which he ate with grits.

The tail and backbone were cooked with dried peas or beans. Some of my brothers even liked the pig feet. Sometimes certain parts were made into souse. I remember the taste as being somewhat sour. It was nothing special in my opinion. Mom would even cook the chitlins for anyone who liked them. They smelled awfully strong (stunk).

Salley, South Carolina, a small town south of Swansea, hosts the well-known "Chitlin Strut" festival yearly. The hoisted hog was carried to a large outdoor table to be cut into parts. Dad and his helpers cut the front legs, which he called shoulders, and the hind legs were the hams. There were ribs, pork chops, streak of lean, fatback. It is hard to remember all the parts. The meat was salt cured in the smokehouse, which was the left wing of the hay barn. This meat lasted for months. The sausages and liver pudding were also stored for later. Once the major part of butchering was over, the fat used to make lard was cooked in the large washpot. This lard was used in the basic cooking for a large family. The men, who helped butcher, were given some meat to take home.

Some of my friends liked to eat at our home because they liked the ham and red-eye gravy for breakfast. We used the fatback for cooking vegetables. I enjoyed the liver pudding with grits and eggs. Sausage with steaming grits was a treat on a cold winter morning. Some of my siblings liked bacon or streak of lean on a biscuit.

As the older hogs were butchered, the sows were bred and raised young piglets. We always had new animals growing in the pens. The cycle continued. The fact that we grew the corn and other grains made the cost factor low for meats. Our dad did not like for us to get too attached to a certain animal because his goal was to eat them.

The Milk Cow

A cow is the mature female of domestic cattle valued for its milk. Her counterpart male animal is the bull. Our cow was a Guernsey breed, a pale yellowish-brown in color. There is dairy farming in every state of the U.S. Many farmers raise cows for the income from their milk. We had only one cow at a given time. We did not raise cattle for money.

The cow stall was a separate building near the pigpen. Her stall was a plain, unpainted building with a tin roof. It was away from the house, because the manure that accumulated smelled bad. Her bed was straw from wheat or oats. A feed trough was just inside on the wall, where we fed her oat grains or shelled corn. A large bucket was used for watering.

Our cost for feeding the cow was minimal, because we raised all her food. Nothing was wasted from our grain crops. The method of separating corn grains from the corncob was fascinating to me. The corn was taken from the cob by an odd piece of equipment called a corn sheller. It was composed of a three- or four-foot-long wooden box with a metal compartment had an attached handle to turn for grinding. The metal compartment had teeth that stripped the grains from the cob. We used the same separating process for the corn that we sent to the milling company for grinding into meal and grits.

Every morning and late evening, the cow had to be milked. The cow's udder sagged when it became full of milk. I am sure it made her teats feel sore. Nature is really smart after all.

My sister Dorcas or my mother usually milked the cow. The milk was strained through cheese cloth over a large mouth jar to make sure no trash was in the milk. Our milk was kept in the cold-water spring on our property or in the old ice box. After the cream came to the top of the containers, it was skimmed off and put into a separate container.

Someone in the family would churn the cream to make homemade butter. The family thought that was "good eating," even though the fat level was not healthy. We even drank the buttermilk. The regular milk and the buttermilk were used in cooking.

Most good cooks who make biscuits regularly prefer to use buttermilk in the dough.

All of my sisters knew how to make biscuits; however, once I left my parents' home, I did not feel it was worth the effort. My personal oven was not heated for two people. My sister-in-law, Edna, became well known for her baking skills. In the early years at Pineview Elementary School as lunchroom manager, she personally made biscuits for the entire school of three to four hundred children. People all around praised her expertise in cooking for a great number.

At our house, we usually drank milk or water with meals. Homemade butter was spread on the homemade bread, biscuits, or corn bread, along with our jellies, jam, or preserves. Any milk left for an extended period was given to the dogs, cats, or pigs.

One chore that no one particularly liked was cleaning out the stall. As with the chicken coop and the hogs' sty manure, the cow's manure was spread over a field for fertilizer. New grain straw was put on the bottom of the stall for the cow to sleep on. Because we did not raise cattle for money, we kept only one cow at a time.

In good weather our cow was put in a pasture with the horses or tied by a long rope so she could graze on the grass or grain left in the field. Cows will eat almost anything horses will eat. One thing I am not sure about—I am unable to remember feeding hay to the cow. Maybe she got enough grass to eat and did not need the hay. My memory is very clear on the genuine contentment of this animal, eating grass and mooing while butterflies flew all around us. Watching a cow can be fun. Lying on the ground tending the cow gives a child time to dream or plan. Those days of watching are still precious me and so are the dreams of better things to come!

Food from the Wild

The men in our family were hunters and/or fishermen in their spare time. Not only did they like to hunt and fish, but they liked to eat what they killed or brought to the shore on their expeditions. My only brother who was not a hunter was Jeremiah. He may have enjoyed hunting, but due to his afflictions, he seldom went into the woods.

Hunting is the sport of capturing or killing wild animals. At one time, man could get his food only if he hunted for it. In my lifetime, most people hunted because they enjoyed it as a sport. A lot of people do not like to hunt because they dislike killing wild animals. For most genuine hunters, the capturing or killing in itself is not so important, because they receive most of their satisfaction from outsmarting the animals they are hunting. Real hunting is a contest between the hunter and the hunted. Weapons give the hunter an advantage over the hunted. However, the animals also have advantages. For a few examples, they run faster, they know the woods, and they can smell and hear better. A good hunter cannot depend only on his weapons; he must know the habits of the game he is hunting. My brothers enjoyed the sport, not only for the food value, but it took them outdoors and gave them the chance to learn the habits of the wild creatures.

Cottontail rabbits were favorite game in our family. A rabbit is a burrowing mammal of the hare family but smaller than most hares. It is characterized by soft fur, long ears, and a stubby tail. Many times my brothers would set traps to catch them alive. A rabbit trap is a strange-looking box about two feet long, six or eight inches wide, and approximately ten inches high. Special treats that rabbits liked were put inside the trap. The treat was a carrot, some lettuce, or an apple. There was a lever rigged through the roof that would automatically close the door when an animal tripped it from inside the box. Sometimes they would hunt rabbits with dogs. These rabbits were brought home and skinned and all the insides were removed. This meat was parboiled to make it very tender. After it was salted and peppered, it was floured like chicken and fried. The meat is quite tasty; it is somewhat like fried chicken but tastes sweeter.

Several different types of squirrels were hunted. The most common ones in our area were the gray and the fox squirrels. They are tree-dwelling rodents (I do not like to think this is true) with heavy fur and long, bushy tails. Squirrels eat nuts and seeds. The men usually hunted them with the dogs. We always had hunting dogs, hounds, beagles, or retrievers. A dog was trained to follow the scent of the hunted until it was chased up a tree. At that point the hunter shot the squirrel with his gun or rifle. When the hunt was over, the men would dress their catch and cook it similar to the way they did the rabbits. When a large number was killed at once, Mom sometimes boiled them, took out all bones, and made dumplings.

Some night hunts could end in a raccoon chase. The raccoon is a small, tree-climbing, flesh-eating mammal. It is characterized by long yellowish gray fur, black masklike markings across the eyes, and a long, black-ringed tail. The hunting dogs could chase a raccoon for a long period of time before it finally wore itself out or felt cornered and climbed a tree. The hunters followed the sound of the dogs barking until the treed animal was located. This could take some time using flashlights and lanterns. Most anyone would think that the raccoon must be a great creature after such an effort to find one. Our hunters would shoot the animal using a flashlight as a guide. The bagged animal would be skinned the next morning and fed to the hunting dogs.

On an unlucky night, the dogs could smell a fox nearby and start a lengthy chase. The fox belongs to the dog family. The most common ones in South Carolina are reddish-brown or gray with bushy tails. A fox is sly and can run for miles and/or hours. Our men were not too anxious to go on a fox chase. Should one be caught or killed, it was fed to the dogs. Many times hunters from other communities would hunt for fox in our area. We could expect a sleepless night when they came to hunt in our woods. Some men have specifically trained dogs for fox hunting. A fox does not give up easily and the chase becomes a battle of endurance. Some hunters get their thrills in an endurance battle.

My dad and older brothers liked to hunt birds in their season. They liked to hunt for partridges (bob-white). This bird has markings of brown and white on a gray body. It is really a small Northern American quail. Our hunters also killed other edible birds in season. Whatever birds were killed were cleaned, fried, and eaten. I always felt that eating these small, beautiful creatures didn't feel right.

Fishing on our farm was limited. The men liked to fish in the creek at night. Sometimes Ezra and Jeremiah would set out fishing poles and check on their catch in the early morning. This is an easy way to get catfish. Catfish is good fried or in a stew. Most of the fish the boys caught near home were perch. These guys were happy to catch anything. Whatever was caught was eaten unless it was a mudfish. They always fished with a cane and line. Their bait was usually earthworms dug up on the farm or caterpillar worms grown on a special tree that attracted these hairy worms. My skin crawls at the thought of touching these ugly, ugly worms. Some of my brothers would spear large bullfrogs after a huge rainstorm. One of our neighbors, Mr. Dykes, wanted the frogs. He ate the frog legs and said they were tasty.

Fruit from the Wild

Isn't it strange with all the peach, apple, plum, and pear trees, we would go looking in the woods and terraces for wild berries? Since our property had a lot of water nearby, wild berries were plentiful. In late June and early July, we enjoyed scrounging for blackberries in the neighborhood. On the property line with a barbwire fence between the Whitaker property and our upper field, we could always find berries growing. Blackberries grew near our house on some of the terraces that were not cleared deliberately.

We children got all bundled up when we went to pick blackberries, because the stalks or vines are very thorny. Blackberry picking was always a real adventure for anyone, especially for a bunch of kids. Not only does the plant have many thorns, but they also attract chiggers (red bugs). If we could remember, we put sulfur around our wrists and shoe tops before leaving the house. Sulfur helped ward off the red bugs. A chigger is a tiny six-legged mite. It causes intense irritating itching when lodged on the skin. This insect is so small it is barely visible to the eye; however, its bite is powerful. Another thing we had to be careful about was rattlesnakes. These snakes were plentiful in our area.

All of the family liked blackberry cobbler and blackberry jelly. The berries that were not eaten immediately were canned for the winter. The jelly made from blackberries was so delicious. The berries were cooked with very little water until they were falling into small pieces. They were then strained several times through cheese cloth to be sure there were no seeds or bulk left in the fruit juice. The juice was boiled with about as much sugar as juice. Certo or SureJel was added to make the juice thicken (jell). It was poured into pint or half-pint jars and sealed. This jelly is my all-time favorite.

Mom's blackberry cobbler was something worth writing about! Those crunchy crusts on top of delicious fruit were mouth-watering, to say the least. Some folks didn't like the seeds, but they never bothered me.

Gooseberries ripen in August. The bushes are spiny shrubs. They were easier to pick but had more risk for snakes in the "dog days" of August. Gooseberries are small, somewhat like the blueberry, but grow closer to the ground. Extreme care must be taken while searching for gooseberries due to the fact that they grow in the woods instead of the fields and open spaces like blackberries. I remember going to pick gooseberries with my two younger siblings in the pine trees behind the Whitaker house, and I stepped right over a water moccasin. We were so frightened that we all ran back home with empty buckets. Pies or no pies, we were done for that day!

Many people talk about the lazy days of summer. Our days were seldom lazy. We had to prepare for the winter long before it arrived, if we wanted to have plenty to eat. By no means am I saying that we had no fun, but rather that the fruit or crop must be gathered when it is ready. It is useless to look after the harvest has passed. We knew blackberries ripen in June not in July!

Chapter 18

GROWING AND PRESERVING

Sweet Potatoes - A Main Food

THE SWEET POTATO is a vegetable that belongs to the morning-glory family of plants. Many times sweet potatoes are called yams; however, yams belong to another family that grows mostly in the tropical regions. Yellow sweet potatoes are mostly grown in the deep south. There are several different types; we grew the ones that had purple-like vines and large leaves. The vines grow from the main stem and lie along the ground.

Dad bought the plants or slips from a seed or plant company. They grew from roots placed in moist, warm, and sandy soil in a hotbed about four weeks before planting time. The stem buds (eyes) from the roots produce the new plants that push up through the soil. These new plants were pulled up and bunched in groups of twenty-five up to one hundred plants per bunch.

One of the men prepared the rows about three or four feet apart. Manure or some type of fertilizer was put into the trenches before rows were made into ridges. The ridge or mound effect helped the water to drain away from the plants. The young slips were planted about twelve inches apart, usually in June. We dug the holes with a hoe and inserted the young plants and packed the soil around them. Next we watered the plants by hand for a few days until they became established. We always hoed any weeds or grass away from the small plants. The men would plow the rows until the vines started running and became too large to get near the base of the plant. At that point we just let the vines grow for the rest of the summer.

The potato crop was harvested in October before the first frost. Our dad would plow down the center of the row and turn the potatoes on top of the soil. We gathered the potatoes into large sacks and brought them to a central location for storing.

The most fascinating part of the process was building the "potato banks." First a round hole was dug into the ground a couple of feet deep. In the hole, new pine straw was put in the bottom a few inches in depth. The men would take timbers about four or five feet in length and form a cone- shaped mound. The freshly harvested potatoes were placed on top of the pine straw in the hole. Potatoes were placed in the hole all the way up to the apex or crown of the cone. More straw was placed on top of the boards, then dirt was piled several inches thick on top of the potato bank. The potato bank prevented the potatoes from freezing during the cold winter. We left a small opening on one side of the mound for retrieving the potatoes. The small opening was covered with a thick board. Any potato with a cut or bruise was held out for early eating.

We always had baked sweet potatoes ready to eat at a moment's notice. Mom always baked a peck or half-bushel at one time. She kept the potatoes for snacking in the warming closet on the top of the wood stove. These potatoes were very healthy, furnishing vitamins A and C plus other nutrients. We did not realize how healthy we were eating at that time. These potatoes were eaten baked, fried, or in potato pie or pones.

They were one of the main staple crops we grew. The whole family liked sweet potatoes.

Cabbage

The cabbage is a common vegetable belonging to the mustard family. It has big, thick leaves formed into a round, compact head on a short, thick stalk. Cabbages were first grown in England and northwestern France but are now grown throughout Europe, Asia, and North America. Other vegetables related to the cabbage include cauliflower, brussels sprouts, broccoli, and turnips. The three kinds of cabbage are white, red, and savoy.

The most popular type in the United States is the white cabbage. It has pale green leaves. We ate it raw as a salad (slaw), cooked as a hot vegetable, or pickled as homemade sauerkraut. Red cabbage, which actually is reddish-purple, can be eaten raw or cooked. It is not as common as the white. The least common is the savoy. Its flavor is good but stronger.

The men tilled an area of the regular garden spot for early spring vegetables in early February. This plot was fertilized with chicken, cow, hog manure, or commercial products. The rows were made about three feet apart. Many farmers plant their seed directly in the field but our family preferred to buy the small plants rather than grow them in flats. In mid-February, we dug holes in the bedded rows about twelve inches apart and put a seedling in each hole. The plants were manually watered until we were sure the plant had taken root. Any time the plant was transplanted, it had to re-establish itself.

Any weeds that came up were chopped down with a hoe and plowed often to keep fresh soil near the base of the plants. This process continued until the plants became so big that the plow would interfere with the growth of the plants. At that point, cultivation ceased and we watched them grow. Usually, by late April or early May, our cabbage was beginning to make heads. The leaves grew into a tight ball. We were anxious to try our first cabbage for the season. Most of the heads of cabbage were mature at about the same time but would continue to grow for several weeks when the weather was good.

It was always tasty cooked in a large iron pot with fatback or bacon and served with hot corn bread. Mom also made slaw to eat with other vegetables and meats. Her slaw was not like I make today. She made it with seasoning and put hot oil over it. Her cooking was good but old-fashioned. When cabbage was left in the garden too long, a large stem or stalk would sprout out of the center of the head. This stalk would bloom and make seeds. At that point the cabbage was no longer edible. About the time seeding began, we had an alternate plan ready. We made sauerkraut.

Making sauerkraut was really a pickling process. All of the mature cabbages were cut from the stalk and put in large tubs or baskets and taken from the field to an area dedicated to this purpose. We had a long outdoor table under chinaberry trees, where much of our food preparation was done. The outer leaves were removed and the cabbage was thoroughly cleaned. Those who were good with butcher knives were assigned to the cutting spot. The tubs of cabbage were cut finely or in shred. Large kegs or open-mouth crocks were filled with the cut cabbages and pressed tightly into the kegs or crocks with a wooden "stomper." The cabbages were salted and water put over the mixture. My parents put a heavy stone on top of each container in order to keep the cabbages under the water while they fermented. An unmistakable aroma or odor came from the fermenting process. The disagreeable odor brought about a heavenly result to the taste buds.

The homemade kraut was packed into glass jars and sealed. The jars were cooked in a large pot of water on the stove for ten minutes or more. This process would preserve the kraut for months to come. Our kraut was served with sausage or spareribs, or cooked with corn bread dumplings. Sauerkraut purchased from the store is good; however, it never will compare favorably with that made with our hands. What we considered to be poor farm family food has now become a specialty in some stores. A few years ago, we went to an October Fest in Helen, Georgia, where large quantities of kraut were sold all week long. People from everywhere wanted to taste it. In our generation, it was one of many survival foods.

The Collard

The collard plant belongs to the mustard family and is related to the cabbage. It resembles kale, but it grows in a warmer climate. It is usually grown in the southern United States. A collard plant will grow to a height of two to four feet tall. The leaves are large. They provide a rich source of vitamin A and other nutrients.

Our collards were farmed very much like our cabbage. The rows were three feet apart. We planted the collard plants farther apart on the rows, because they grew much larger than the cabbage plants. Our family planted collards in late August with the expectation to start harvesting the crop in October. We thought they tasted better after the first frost. The frost seemed to calm the tartness of flavor somewhat.

Each leaf had to be checked for insects or worms before it was ready to be cooked. Its leaves are not in a head like the cabbage. The person preparing the collards for cooking stacked a number of leaves together and sliced the leaves about ¼ inch wide. A whole bunch of the greens were prepared at one time for cooking. We cooked them in water with salt and bacon drippings. Mom served them with baked sweet potatoes and corn bread. Many people put sugar in them while cooking them. I prefer mine plain.

As a child, I did not realize just how healthy our family ate. Our most basic foods were very good for everyone. The only way we compromised the quality was with the seasoning. Kraut could be made from collards exactly like cabbage and canned in jars.

Winter Gardening

Our winter garden usually consisted of Irish potatoes, English (sweet) peas, onion, and cabbage. Around February 14, the men tilled a garden spot for early crops. The area was fertilized with chicken, cow, or hog manure, or sometimes with commercial products. The rows were approximately three feet apart. Each vegetable was planted in its own unique way. These vegetables were very tolerant of cold and would be planted as soon as the overall condition of the soil permitted. Mid-February was about six weeks before the last expected frost.

Irish potato (red potato or white potato) seeds are actually eyes from special seeding potatoes bought from a feed and seed store. The new growth is the potato seeds. The eyes were cut from the potato with a sharp knife. Enough of the potato was left under each eye to give it a good start in establishing itself as a new plant. We dug holes in the bedded rows about twelve inches apart and put an eye in each hole. The new seedling would sprout and become visible above the soil in about a week to ten days. There was not much grass or weeds this early in the season; however, any weeds that appeared were chopped down with a hoe. The new plants were plowed often to keep the fresh soil around the base of the plants. The plowing continued frequently until the plants became too large to get near their base.

The latter part of April or early May, the plant would produce many small white blooms. Shortly thereafter, once the blossoms began to fall off the plant, the new potatoes were ready for harvest. Someone in our family would use a sweep (special plow) and plow down the center of the rows. This process would turn the fresh crop on top of the ground. The children would go down each row and pick up the new potatoes in buckets. We would bring them to a central location for culling. Any potatoes with cuts, bruises, or bad spots were separated from the ones without flaws. The better ones were stored in a barn on a burlap sheet. They would remain good like this for many weeks. The potatoes with cuts were taken to the kitchen for quick cooking.

Our family enjoyed the potatoes stewed, baked, or as potato salad. It was rare for us to eat French fries. I remember new red potatoes cooked with string beans. One of my favorite meals was beef stew with new potatoes and onions.

English (sweet) peas were planted about the same time as the Irish potatoes. Some claim St. Patrick's Day was the ideal time for sweet peas, but a few days either way did not make any difference. The ground was prepared the same as for the Irish potato, and we usually planted them near each other. Holes were dug with a hoe in the ridge of the three feet rows about a foot apart. Three or four seeds were dropped in each hole. We purchased the seeds from a feed and seed store or ordered them from a seed catalog.

Once the seed germinated in a week, more or less, the rows were cultivated the same as other vegetables. In a few weeks, the small plant would get runners and had to be staked. Thin slats or small branches (limbs), four or five feet tall, were placed at each hill of peas. With proper care the vines clung to the stakes and grew quickly. In early April, the crop of peas was ready to eat. Sometimes, we cooked the whole young pod.

The pods become tough if not picked early. Early English peas were very tasty cooked with a little water, salt, and butter.

Spring onions were planted at the same time as the English peas. They were fairly resistant to the cold temperatures. Sets were bought each year for planting. A set is a young bulb ready for planting. Sets actually grow on a spire that grows out of an onion left too long in the field. A matured onion plant grew a spire in its center somewhat like a cabbage.

We dug holes a couple of inches deep and six to eight inches apart. The sets can be planted close and thinned out by pulling every other plant to eat as a green onion. The remaining plants were left until maturity. These green onions were very good with other vegetables or salad.

Early Spring Gardening

On our farm the early spring gardening consisted of radish, lettuce, carrot, beets, sweet corn, and mustard greens. These vegetables were planted about two to four weeks before the last expected frost. These vegetables were more tolerant to the cool nights than our regular spring crops. Many of the seeds were ordered from a catalog during the winter months when there was more available spare time. The seeds that could not be ordered were purchased at a local store usually where commercial fertilizers were sold. In early March, the men tilled the soil and fertilized the area the same as the winter crops. After the rows were made and the ridges over the fertilizer were prepared, the girls were ready to plant our seeds.

All the early spring vegetable seeds were planted in the same manner. A half-inch to one-inch trench was run down the center of the built-up ridge. The small seeds were planted very close together. Some would say we sowed them, but not quite that close. With the exception of the sweet corn, the seeds were small. We planted a row of each, except for the corn. The seeds were placed by hand into the small trench dug with our hoe. The seeds were carefully covered with a garden rake. The sweet corn was planted with the hoe about a foot apart. Our corn seeds were covered with the hoe as we dropped the seeds into the ground. Most of the time the sweet corn was planted with the regular spring planting in April. Usually, we planted a few rows of the early corn.

When the small plants germinated, they were thinned if they appeared too thick to reach maturity. The radishes and carrots have such small roots, they require little thinning. The beets have larger bottoms and require three to five inches growing space. Lettuce and mustard greens were left fairly close together. All of these seeds would be up in a week to ten days. After the seedlings were up, weed control was the most important job. A lot of it was done with a hoe. Our family plowed the plants until they started to get big. In about six weeks from planting these vegetables, they were ready to be eaten. Our family liked to eat them.

Probably the worst enemy of the early grown vegetables was rabbits. They loved our lettuce and carrots. Sometimes aphids or rust might attack the young plants. Should this occur, we sprayed them with malathion or another chemical.

Most of these vegetables were eaten or given to family, friends, or neighbors as they were harvested. The beets were an exception; we pickled them for wintertime eating. Beet tops were also edible, but we never cooked them. Traditions run strong in some areas. Pickling the beets was simple. We boiled the beets in their skins until the skins would slide off the beet. After taking them from the boiling water, we quickly dipped them in cold water and the peelings slipped right off. This method preserved the rich purple color. We cut them in ½ inch slices, put them into a large canning pot and covered them with sugar, vinegar and pickling spice. As soon as they started to boil, we put them into quart jars and sealed them immediately. Pickled beets are beautiful.

Summer Garden

The vegetables that were sensitive to cool temperatures were planted on Good Friday on our family farm. Some of the vegetables included snap beans, squash, tomatoes, peppers, cucumber, and cantaloupes. If the soil was warm enough, we planted lima beans and eggplants. Whenever the soil was cold at night, we waited a couple weeks to plant lima beans, eggplants, and melons. Good Friday was a special day for our gardens. Hopefully by that day the frosts were over. Sometimes Easter came in late March or early April when there was a probability of frost; in that situation, we waited a few more weeks for the more sensitive plants.

The plot chosen for a summer garden was tilled and fertilized as were the winter garden and early spring garden. The rows were spaced about three to four feet apart for most plants with the exceptions of cucumbers and melons. They required more room since they grew on vines. Once the rows with their ridges were prepared, the girls were ready to plant the seeds.

Seeds for the garden were ordered from a catalog or purchased from the feed and seed store. We always had the seeds ready for Good Friday planting. The snap beans were either bush beans or Kentucky Wonders (pole beans). Holes, about one foot apart, were dug with a hoe in the ridge on top of the row for bush beans, pole beans, and lima beans. Three or four seeds were dropped into each hole and covered with the hoe. We usually planted a couple of rows of each type of bean to be sure we had an ample supply for our extra-large family. The small plants would be up and growing in about a week unless the nights were too cool. We were anxious to see how well the plants would grow.

Watching for new growth was an exciting time for young children after they worked hard. The holes for squash were dug about three feet apart, because the plant gets large quickly. Squash seeds for white or yellow squash were planted exactly as the bean seeds. The rows for cucumbers and cantaloupes would be spaced farther apart, because their vines spread several feet from their roots. Cucumber and cantaloupe seeds were planted three or four feet apart by digging a hole with the hoe and dropping three or four seeds in each hill. The men plowed the rows until the plants grew too large. The girls used a hoe to chop any weeds or grass growing between the plants. In about six weeks from planting these vegetables, we were eating fresh vegetables. We usually planted the cantaloupes some distance from our cucumbers so they would not pollinate. Cantaloupes that are mixed with cucumbers taste bad. We enjoyed having fresh melons for breakfast.

When planting tomatoes, peppers, and eggplants, our family usually bought the seedlings from the feed and seed store rather than planting seeds early in a hotbed. The plants were purchased in a bundle of fifty to one hundred plants. We normally planted several rows of tomatoes and maybe one row of different types of peppers. Just a few eggplants were enough for our family because they produced a lot of fruit per plant. All of these seedlings were placed in a hole dug with a hoe about three inches deep. The plants were set out twelve to eighteen inches apart on the ridge made by the men when they drew and fertilized the rows. Once the seedlings were planted, they were watered manually until they took root. In six to eight weeks, the vegetables were ready to pick.

Tomatoes were an important part of our family's diet. We ate them raw, fried as green tomatoes, and in soups, especially corn, okra, and tomatoes. Let me tell you more in the canning section of this chapter. My dad ate hot peppers with all vegetables.

Garden peas were usually planted along with the other summer crops in April. They were planted and cultivated in the same way. One thing different was that we saved our pea seeds from year to year. My family planted two different kinds of peas in our garden—Cheney and pink eye (similar to black-eyes). In about six weeks, we had plenty of peas to eat and to be canned. Another way we planted peas was between the cornstalks in the large cornfield. They were regular field peas. Sometimes Dad sowed peas in a large field and cut them as hay. Peas were a staple food item in summer and dried in the winter months. We shelled and snapped peas for canning for winter.

Okra was sensitive to cold and the time for planting was after the soil was warm. The okra seeds were very hard and germinated slowly. Our family soaked the seeds in warm water for a couple of days before planting. The rows were made and fertilized as the other vegetables. The seeds were dropped into holes dug two to three inches deep and about eighteen inches apart. In a week to ten days, the plants would be up and starting to grow. It would be June or early July before the pods grew, but once they started producing, the plants would produce pods until frost. The blossoms were beautiful and edible. One must be careful when gathering okra, because the stalks and leaves caused one to itch. Okra plants and pods have spines on them.

Our family cooked okra many ways. It was somewhat slimy when stewed. Many people do not like it stewed, but I really liked it any way it was cooked. My mother cut okra crosswise the pod, battered it and fried it. Fried okra is quite tasty. We also boiled it whole on top of green peas or butter beans with bacon drippings. This was probably my favorite way to eat okra. We cooked it with corn and tomatoes. We canned a lot of okra this way.

Other Trees and Plants We Grew

There were some other fruits and nuts that we grew and ate. Strawberry plants were perennials on our farm. We had a small area that was set aside for strawberries. They were ripe in early April and eaten by the family almost as soon as they were picked.

We had several types of grapes on the farm. There was a large arbor of concord grapes that grew in bunches. We also had regular muscadines (wild grapes). These were eaten from the vines and made into delicious jellies. The fruit trees grown included several different apples, figs, peaches, and plums. Kleckley Farm was near our home and grew fruit for sale. Peaches were abundant there. Their prices were good, especially if the buyer would pick them and furnish the baskets.

We had some hazelnut and walnut trees. Hickory nuts grew in the woods, but they were very hard and difficult to crack. We ate hickory nuts just for our own pleasure. Our farm had yellow apples that ripened in May or early June and large reddish apples that ripened in September. Apples were eaten from the tree, baked in cobblers, or canned for winter. The peaches were eaten very much like the apples. Sometimes we made peach pickles from cling-seed peaches. Plums were eaten fresh from the tree or canned as plum jelly. Hazelnuts were small and hard to extract from the shells. Therefore, you ate what you were willing to work hard to get from the shells. Walnuts were not too different from hazel nuts as to getting the meat of the nuts. However, sometimes we extracted them from the shells for a special dish. We never seemed to get a lot of figs from our tree. They were more difficult to grow than other fruit trees. The ones we gathered we either ate raw or made fig preserves. Fig preserves were really tasty on warm bread with butter.

Canning for the Winter

Once school was out at the end of May, preserving of the fruits and vegetables really geared up. We worked hard trying to prepare for the winter months by canning the fresh produce as it became available. Our big family ate much of the fruits and vegetables as they ripened. Mom and the older children cleaned and washed jars before the season rush began. New lids or caps were purchased before needed.

Green beans were probably the earliest vegetable ready for canning. Snap beans were one of the easiest things to can. We snapped off the ends of the bean and broke it into one- to two-inch pieces. Pole beans have string (hair like formation) growing down the side of them. While snapping them, we pulled the strings off. The beans were washed carefully to make sure there was no dust or sprays on them. The beans were cooked a few minutes in a large broiler (sixteen-quart canning pot). This made them tender. Next, clean quart jars were stuffed with the hot beans. About one-half teaspoon of salt was put on top of the beans in the jars and covered with liquid. The sealed jars were cooked in a hot-water bath for about twenty minutes in a hard boil. This process ensured that they would not spoil. They were taken from the boiler and made sure the lids were screwed tightly.

Canning fresh sweet corn was time-consuming. The ears had to be cleaned as soon as possible after plucking them from the plant. Sweet corn loses its delicate flavor if not used quickly or refrigerated. Our method included several helpers. The first person removed the shucks and another picked out the silks from the cobs. The last person cut the kernels from the cob and scraped the cob to get the sweet juice. The kernels and juice were packed into the clean quart jars. We put one half teaspoon salt on top of the corn. We made sure the grains were covered with juice or water before putting into the hot-water bath. The jars were boiled about fifteen to twenty minutes.

A person who is willing to pick and shell lima beans must really like them or is very willing to work extremely hard to eat fresh vegetables. Lima/butterbeans grow really low to the ground. It is extremely hard to stoop that low to pick them from their vines. As I grew older, I told my friends that I only picked these beans for love. I really loved my family. We children were not asked if we liked to pick but were told we must help with the picking.

When shelling lima beans, anyone who was not working on something else was expected to shell beans. The canning process was simple. After the beans were shelled, they were washed several times to be certain there was no sand or trash on the beans. The fresh beans were packed in clean jars. Salt and water to cover were added, and the jars went into the hot water bath. After cooking about thirty minutes, we removed them from the water and stored them for winter.

Picking and shelling peas is much easier than lima beans. Peas pods grow in a cluster; therefore, a handful could be picked at once. In a short time a basket would be filled with fresh peas. Shelling was easy. The pea shells are longer and produce more for less effort. Sometimes my mother cooked the peas in a large pot, then filled the jars and sealed them. Any time the jars were not going to be boiled, the lids were preheated, because they sealed better. Most often we used the hot-water bath here, too.

Tomatoes were canned in several ways on our farm. It was fun picking tomatoes. In a short time, a bushel basket would be full of juicy tomatoes. We canned them by the bushel. Our family usually peeled the skins from the tomatoes. However, I learned a much easier way since leaving my parents' home. I scald them in hot water for a few seconds and remove the skins in a jiffy. As a child, after peeling the tomato, we cut it into quarters. The tomatoes that were canned alone were dropped into a large canning pot.

Salt was added to the pot of tomatoes. They were boiled about ten to fifteen minutes, after which they were poured into quart jars and sealed. Tomatoes seemed to do well canned alone. Many times we canned corn, okra, and tomatoes together. This made great soup in the winter months. Sometimes we canned okra and tomatoes or tomatoes and corn. Canned tomatoes alone or with corn and okra looked great in a jar. They were simple to can.

Our family rarely canned squash because of its soft texture. It does not seem to hold up well. Now cucumber pickles were the way to go with "cukes." We made three different types—bread and butter, sour pickles, and crispy sweet pickles. These are my all-time favorite. Since my family and I like sweet crisp cucumber pickles so much, let me tell you how to make them.

- Wash 7 pounds of long slender cucumbers.

- Cut them crosswise into ¼ inch or less pieces.

- Soak in lime water 24 hours.

- Use 3 cups of lime to 2 gallons water, in a very large bucket or pot. (Lime is lime no matter where you buy it, but much cheaper when bought in a large quantity from hardware store or feed and seed store.)

- After 24 hours, remove the crisp cucumbers from the lime water and put in fresh clean water. (I use one of my sink's bins.)

- Change to clean water every hour for 4 hours.

- Wash and drain; be careful not to break the slices.

- Put the crisp slices in a large canning pot. Combine 3 pints white vinegar, ½ box pickling spice (put in bag made from thin cloth), and 5 pounds of sugar. Soak overnight in this solution.

- Cook at boiling point 1 hour, but do not let boil (simmer). Put in clear jars and seal.

The cooking process will make them bright green. Before I open a jar, I put it in the refrigerator. These pickles are delicious in slaw and many salads or by themselves.

Mom pickled hot peppers for my dad. She boiled them in vinegar and water before putting them in pint jars. They were sealed in hot jars with caps.

We canned peaches, apples, and pears as we did vegetables. Any fruit that was not eaten fresh or in cobblers was canned. The fruit was peeled and taken from the core or the seed. It was cut into small chunks, put into a large canning pot, a little sugar was added and enough water to cover it. Then it was cooked until tender, about fifteen minutes. We filled clean jars with the fruit, making sure it was covered with the liquid. The hot jars were sealed with warm caps, and sometimes they were inverted during the cooling process, which made sealing absolutely certain.

Jelly was made from grapes, plums, and blackberries in our home. Each of these fruits was cooked a long time to remove the juice from the pulp. The juice was strained several times to be sure it was clear of pulp. The juice was mixed with sugar and Pepin (Sure-jell or Certo) and cooked according to the recipe. We used pint or half-pint jars.

Homemade fig preserves and watermelon preserves were wonderful in hot biscuits. Preserves were made somewhat like jellies except the fruit is well cooked and left in the mixture of sugar and Certo. My childhood home was filled with food that we canned, which made it possible to survive during the hard, cold winters. Canning fruits and vegetables was a real part of our existence. Children in my generation learned survival skills at a young age. As an adult, I have received many awards for my canning, exhibited at the South Carolina State Fair and at BellSouth Telephone Pioneer Conventions.

While attending Southern Wesleyan University in 1993, I did a portfolio assessment program to earn thirteen hours of credits. This program allowed me to earn academic credit for college-level learning gained through life experiences. These credit hours saved me many hours of Saturday classes in order to get my elective hours.

Sugar Cane - Our Most Unusual Plant

Sugar cane was the most unusual plant that I can remember growing on the Busbee farm. We did not always grow it; however, my memory is very clear on the process. In reviewing the history of sugar cane, I found that it was grown all the way back to Alexander the Great about 325 BC. Christopher Columbus is credited with bringing it to the western hemisphere on his second voyage. This may be the prime reason that it is a main crop in Cuba and other Caribbean Islands.

Sugar cane typically grows in tropical or subtropical climates. Fertile soil that holds a lot of moisture is best for sugar cane growing. That is why Hawaii, Florida, and Louisiana (swampy territories) are known for their yielding good crops. Our family property had Bull Swamp Creek as a boundary and also had another stream going through the center of a wooded area. It was near the stream that my dad chose to grow his sugar cane. The soil was always moist and seemed to grow most anything.

Rows were spaced five feet or more apart. Sugar cane was grown from stem cuttings. A stalk was cut into short pieces, each bearing a node, and laid in the furrows and covered with fertilizer and soil. The new growth (stalks) grew from the joints of the old cane. In a fairly short time, the buds on the nodes swelled and burst open. New stalks appeared from the soil. Shortly, thereafter, leaves appeared. In a couple of weeks the stalk developed nodes and internodes. The stalks would grow seven to fifteen feet high, and two inches to five inches in diameter.

The stalks had no branches but had long, narrow leaves arranged in two rows. Cane stalks were divided into sections, somewhat like a bamboo cane. (Fishing poles are made from bamboo canes.) The sections are called internodes. Small buds, which resemble an Irish potato eye, appeared at these sections. The stem was colored a yellowish-green to somewhat reddish color. I vaguely remember our plants having a slight purple tint. There was not a lot of cultivation in the rows of sugar cane. Soil must be kept moist.

Our cane was cut by hand. The person who cuts the cane by hand uses a large steel knife. It was cut close to the ground and stripped of its leaves with a hook. The top was cut off at the last matured joint. Gathering sugar cane stalks and stripping off its growths was a difficult task. The job required someone who could think ahead and really liked the homemade syrup with biscuits or corn bread. My dad fit the description of that elite group of men. After every meal he wanted syrup on something.

The stalks were gathered in piles and picked up on the wagon or a trailer behind the old car. Dad hauled the stalks to a neighboring farmer who owned a cane mill. This mill equipment was unique in every aspect, so much so that I felt compelled to try to paint you a word picture. Just for you! The contraption had a mule- or horse-pulled motor. The method of making the motor run was most memorable. A shaft came up from the grinding mechanism (motor) and was connected to a large log or long wooden plank. On the end of the log, a mule, in his normal plowing gear, was hooked or attached to the long pole. This animal walked in a complete circle around and around the equipment. A knowledgeable person fed the long cane stalks into an opening in the contraption on the side about midway. As the mule walked in his circle, the sweet liquid was ground from the stalks and flowed into a special container for that unique purpose. This process continued for hours or at least until the cane was all ground. The juice was poured into fresh gallon jugs and carried home for the next step.

Once the juice reached home, it was poured into a very large iron kettle or our iron washpot (same pot used for washing clothes) and boiled for quite a while. The cooking turned the sweet liquid into delicious homemade syrup. Our syrup was sealed in clean glass jugs or gallon jars until needed. The syrup would keep for a long period. This was some of Dad's favorite food.

PART 7

Blessing in Disguise

Chapter 19

REWARDS OF GROWING UP WITHOUT MUCH STUFF

Our family never possessed a great deal of the worldly goods that our city friends or cousins owned. Farming was a way of life. We enjoyed the quiet and peace of the country despite the lack of money. Happiness cannot be purchased.

There was no fear of having someone steal what you worked hard to earn. Our family did not need to lock our doors; however, we usually did lock them when we were gone for a long period. Security was a built-in advantage from the 1940s and 1950s. The men in our family all owned guns for hunting wild game, not for protection. At night our windows were flung open for the cool air with never a fear that someone may do us harm or climb into the home and steal.

Because we had little extra money, there were few bought toys. This fact helped us learn to be creative and gave us the ability to use our imaginations. The innovative approach to creating childhood recreation was carried forward into our adult lives. I have observed creativity in my older siblings. With little formal training as a machinist, my brother Floyd had many opportunities to make the General Electric Plant in Irmo stay operative by his talents. On a number of occasions, an engineer would consult with him to find a way to keep the equipment operating smoothly. Most country people learn to use whatever experiences they have available.

One of the tenets that I hold dear is that hard work builds character. Work gives an individual the moral strength, self-discipline, and the fortitude to do what is right, rather than take the low road whenever the choices are difficult. Many years ago, a friend of mine told me that I had a much stronger constitution than he. For a long time, I was not sure of exactly what he meant. Once the light in my brain came on, it was perfectly clear. Long before I was faced with grappling the temptation at hand, my inner being dictated that I take the high road and stand firm. A strong character will prevent an individual from crossing the threshold of a wrong path or stimulus even though it may appear appealing or exciting.

Our family was close-knit in the early years. There were few distractions such as television, telephones, or loud music. It seems to me that people care more who have fewer things to encumber their lives. We all shared the same radio and listened to the same music, such as the "WIS Hired Hands" (real country music). Our family was less wasteful than most families today. My mother made bread pudding from leftover biscuits. Today her dessert is considered a delicacy in some areas. We ate healthier organic fruits and vegetables. Children were taught to eat whatever was set before them and without any complaining. Life seemed simple back then, or at least less stressful.

Most of my childhood dreams have come to pass. My family and I have traveled a lot in the last several decades. We have visited some of the largest cities on this continent, including New York City, Atlanta, Boston, Los Angeles, Dallas/Fort Worth, and Seattle, as well as Vancouver and Ontario, Canada. We have enjoyed the grandeur of our National Parks, such as the Grand Canyon and Yosemite. We have cruised several times to Nassau in the Bahamas. I have enjoyed the excitement of Hollywood and the New York City Broadway District and dined at the Black Orchid in Honolulu and Emeril's in New Orleans. However, I always remember where my roots developed. While riding down Delarosa Drive in Beverly Hills, California, a few years ago, I could still remember Jones Wire Road in Lexington County, South Carolina. My roots grew deep—*Once Upon a Country Road*.

Afterthoughts

Many things are very different today than in my childhood and youth, and I think you need to know. I fully understand that there are always changes—the only thing that never changes is God's Word and his love for mankind. Moral code, social affairs, technology, and the world's view of life have evolved drastically in my life span. Family values have eroded. This writing is a hodgepodge of things that were relevant in my lifetime.

During World War II and shortly after the end of this great conflict, our military was treated with much more respect and adoration than in later years. Young ladies were invited to the USO, with chaperones, to entertain our young men in the cities, such as our capital city, Columbia, South Carolina. The older women running these institutions became mother figures to our brothers and lonely young guys who were drafted to serve. For many of these fellows, it was the first time that they had been away from their mothers. The girls would dance and share some real talk with some mother's boy.

After the war ended, there was dancing in the streets and an overflowing appreciation for the grit and bravery of our men returning home. Much effort was given to finding jobs for our returnees. In retrospect, our arms were opened with love to World War II warriors.

Children were encouraged to buy U.S. Saving Stamps at the Post Office, and at school on certain days, or the bank. These stamps were posted in a book until $18.75 was saved, then the booklet could be converted into a War Bond to help the government pay for the war. After five years a bond was worth $25.

By the time the Korean conflict occurred, I was starting high school. Our radios were tuned in to the news with great interest. This war (conflict) did not end with an all-out win, but rather a peace treaty or an accord. Many lives were lost for a very real cause; however, there was not a genuine victory. Their coming home was not the hooray that many of these guys expected. Even though some were marred for life with shell shock, wounds, broken bodies, and emotional scars, they were not joyfully received as their earlier cohorts. Many struggled to find jobs and acceptance in a changed environment.

Our Vietnam veterans returned to an unwelcoming country. It was not their choice to fight a losing war. Many were not appreciated for their service to our great country. That war was fought with much disagreement on the home front.

Some children actually went to school barefoot in the 1940s, not because it was fashionable, but rather because they had no good shoes. One must understand wartime was quite difficult for some families. The husbands and sons had to leave home and the mothers and girls had to survive as best they could. Ladies ran businesses and jobs that they knew little about. On farms young kids took on the heavy responsibilities of keeping the land productive. Their teenage years all but evaporated. This generation matured fast.

Holidays were so different back then. Even though we had so little, Mother's Day was a big deal. We wanted to give something. It may have been a spool of thread, a pack of hair pins, a pack of gum, or a homemade card. These things came from the child's heart. Another tradition that meant so much to us was wearing roses. Because our mother was alive, that meant we wore a red rose on our collars or lapels. Others with no living mother wore a white rose. We children watched closely just before that day to make sure our roses were blooming. In other words, we got excited with anticipation, waiting to see if we had roses to express our gratitude to a worthy lady, our mom. It was with sadness that we gave our parents white roses to wear. Traditions die hard in my family, because I still wore my rose for Mother's Day well into the 1960s.

Easter was also a special event; in fact, I probably enjoyed it better than Christmas. We each got a dozen eggs to dye. A day during the week before Easter, Mom boiled ten dozen eggs. She had many different colors of dye and plenty of vinegar ready to put into the many cups or small jars. We had a blast choosing colors and drawing designs. There were egg hunts at school, at church, and around our home. Another important thing, if there was any money, we ordered new clothes from the sales catalogs. The thrill of getting a store-bought outfit was wondrous.

Christmas was not secular in our family. It was all about Jesus's birthday. We got fruit and candy in our hats or bonnets. If we had a tree, it came from the woods and was decorated with homemade paper chains and other homemade things. We had a good meal. Church and school pageants were the real excitement. We worked really hard to make these plays meaningful.

Valentine's Day was special. We spent a lot of time making cards for all our friends, and if we were fortunate enough, we bought cards for everyone. Covering a shoebox or a cigar box with paper and cut-out hearts was the norm. We always put a slit in the top center of our box. The children who had cards for us put them into our box. It was a lot of fun for the little ones. It was only after I left home that I got candy on Valentine's Day.

Even church was different back then. Few small country churches had baptismal pools as today. Our Methodist or Lutheran neighbors did not face a dilemma as other faiths, because they used little water in a font to christen a new believer. New converts from other churches were taken to a pond or river and immerged in water baptism. I was baptized in the Claude Smith Pond a few miles from our house. These baptisms took place only a few times a year. Bible School was much more practical. Our crafts were things made by hand such as bird houses, wooden picture frames, or something that could be used in the home.

During my high school years in the 1950s, girls seldom wore pants and almost never to school or church. Cheerleaders' uniforms covered most of their bodies. They wore saddle oxfords and bobby socks, like most of the girls. The girls who did not wear saddle oxfords wore penny loafers. Penny loafers were brown leather shoes with slots on the top where new pennies were inserted. Crinoline slips were the thing in the mid-1950s. Many in their upper teens wore three or four crinoline slips at one time. Sitting for a long time was not too super. The girls who were rebellious and wanted to express themselves wore peroxide streaks in their hair. Some of my friends put a Toni home permanent in their hair. I never had the nerve to try anything outrageous, because I feared my folks would send me packing. It was really not that bad; however, I had great respect for my parents' wisdom.

The technological changes have far exceeded my wildest dreams or expectations. When I was in school, we were fortunate to have a manual typewriter. Southern Bell used comptometers for all mathematical functions. We finally got a few electric calculators on the floor. These machines were as big as a typewriter and very noisy, but much faster than the manual process on our equipment. One of my early job assignments was posting wire and cable amounts to continuous manuals. The hardest part of this job was to convert linear feet to conductor miles in the cables. This process was handled manually unless we could borrow a noisy calculator. Finally, computer systems came into existence. Our building had almost an entire floor dedicated to the computer room. We did not get personal computers until about 1980.

Back in the 1940s, telephones were a far cry from what we are accustomed to now. The "central office" had a desk called a switchboard. A line from this tiny office ran to Columbia for long distance calls. The local operator connected you to the party with whom you wanted to speak. At first there were no dials on the telephones in the homes. The earliest phone was a box hung on the wall with a receiver. When you wanted to make a call, the operator asked, "Number please?" Just recently, while talking with my investment advisor, I casually told him that when my husband and I moved into our home, we had an eight-party line. He was totally stunned and had never heard of a party line. An eight-party line is a pair of wires in a large cable that serves eight families. Each home had its own distinct ring. All parties on the line got another family's ring in addition to his.

There have been some major changes in the medical profession. My mother had some medical issues in the late 1940s and the early 1950s. Her doctor, Dr. James Fort, would come to our home to check on her. Seldom did she go to his office in North, South Carolina. Some doctors would accept partial payments or even more strange, they would barter with the patient. A few would accept eggs, meat, or homegrown fruit or vegetables in lieu of cash. We rarely went to the doctor's office. In this time span, we had many home remedies. Should we contact pink eye, we wore potato compresses over our eyes. Sweet oil drops were put in the ear should we have an earache. For poison ivy, we were soaked in bleach water and used an over-the-counter lotion. One treatment used turpentine mixed with Vick's salve. After these many years, some things seem vague. Mom rubbed our chests with a homemade concoction whenever we seemed congested and put warm towels around our little bodies.

The care of our sick family members has changed drastically. After my oldest sister, Dorcas, was married and had a couple children, she became very ill for several months. Her husband brought her back to our house so our mother could take care of her. This was not at all unusual but rather the norm in the 1950s. With proper care and the entire family nurturing her, Dorcas made a full recovery. The more scientifically advanced our society becomes, the more we seem to fear and deny the fact of death. When I was a young girl, my grandmother had congestive heart failure. I can remember her in her own home instead of a hospital room. We children gathered around her bed as she shared stories about her past. This old-fashioned custom was repeated all over our neighborhood. The simple fact that my grandmother was never carried out of the home provided her with a familiar environment or less adjustment during the termination of life. I was allowed to remain close and could hear Mother talk about the impending fatality. I believe the sharing involved as an extended family prepared the young children for the eventual death and helped us view death as a part of life.

Over five decades, the way peoples' final rites are handled have changed drastically. In the 1940s and 1950s, the sick person died at home and then a funeral vehicle picked up the corpse. As soon as the body was embalmed, my grandmother was brought home to lie in state for several days. The whole community responded by bringing food and flowers. Someone sat in the same room with the dead person day and night until the time of the funeral. I believe the old traditions helped us cope with the finality of death better than the more recent time where everything has become mechanical and dehumanized. Death or the loss of a loved one is never easy; however, understanding the processes is helpful. Death is as certain as life.

Something happened in my early years that left an indelible mark on my mind. Some of our neighbors had several young children. Their mother had gone nearby to her friend's house briefly. While Dell was gone, her five-year-old, Ernestine, was warming herself in front of the open fireplace when her dress caught fire. The oldest child at home was no more than seven, and there was a younger girl at home too, probably three. They were terrified and ran for their mother. Of course, the five-year-old didn't know about the stop, drop, and roll method of putting out fire. Her burns were so intense that she died. The whole community mourned over such a tragedy. The funeral director, Mr. Thompson, grieved because his child was the same age. I remember telling my mother many times that I wanted to live such a productive life full of goodness that when I died even the funeral director would be sorry. To make this world a better place is still my goal, and I hope that this book will somehow enlighten my readers on how I became who I am today.

Life is wonderful. I shared fifty-one years with my husband who was a constant source of strength and leadership. We were blessed to own a beautiful home, reared a wonderful daughter, and share with so many others along the way, especially children. Most importantly, Christ is the Lord of my life. My philosophy has always been to "give my love freely and something extraordinary will be returned to me." Should you hear that Ruth Busbee Smith has died, don't believe a word of it, because I have just moved to a better world of eternal bliss.

Acknowledgments

McKenzie Grace Pierce, my granddaughter – Her great interest in family history prompted me to venture into the unknown world of book writing.

Pamela S. Pierce, my daughter – She spent countless hours on proofing, editing, and formatting this text with her superb technical skills.

John C. Edwards – I thank him for his genuine belief in my ability to write this book and his final revisions.

David K. Phillips, for his cover art, and Cathleen Ellisor, for her paintings within the book.

Parker Sparrow, Stephanie Stone, and Frances Motte for their editing contributions.

Frances Motte, Loretta Hutto, and Linda Shealy for their encouragement.

Dottie Boatwright for facilitating the Prime Times writing class.

F. Marion Busbee, Wanda K. Busbee, Helen B. Long, and Carolyn R. Sightler for family pictures.

Melba C. Hoover and Rhett Inabinet for their historical contributions.

Loretta Hutto, James T. Busbee, Barbara Hutto Poole, Linda Shealy, and Cindy Leitner for their photos.

Austin Snead, Grace Pierce, Pamela Pierce, and Wanda Busbee for technical support.

Printed in the USA
CPSIA information can be obtained
at www.ICGtesting.com
JSHW072206301223
54590JS00013B/100